Screen
Smart
Children

Screen
Smart
Children

**A Guide to Helping Kids Thrive in a
World That Never Switches Off**

DR MARK WILLIAMS
& GAVIN McCORMACK

**SIMON &
SCHUSTER**

New York · Amsterdam/Antwerp · London · Toronto · Sydney/Melbourne · New Delhi

SCREEN SMART CHILDREN
First published in Australia in 2026 by
Simon & Schuster (Australia) Pty Limited
Level 4, 32 York St, Sydney NSW 2000

10 9 8 7 6 5 4 3 2 1

New York Amsterdam/Antwerp London Toronto Sydney/Melbourne New Delhi
Visit our website at www.simonandschuster.com.au

A catalogue record for this
book is available from the
National Library of Australia

ISBN: 9781761639715

Cover design: Luke Causby/Blue Cork
Illustrations: Elizabeth Kerry
Typeset by Midland Typesetters, Australia
Printed and bound in Australia by Griffin Press

The paper this book is printed on is certified against the
Forest Stewardship Council® Standards. Griffin Press holds
chain of custody certification SCS-COC-001185. FSC®
promotes environmentally responsible, socially beneficial
and economically viable management of the world's forests.

CONTENTS

Introduction

Welcome, fellow parents, caregivers, educators, guard-ians and brave navigators of the digital frontier! If you're reading this book, you've probably found yourself staring at a glowing screen, wondering just how this little device took over your living room, your child's attention and possibly even your dreams. Yes, it's sad but true: most of us see phone notifications in our nightmares these days!

Whether your child is a toddler who could swipe before they could talk, or a teenager who prefers to text rather than speak, you've picked up this book because you care. That's the first and most important step. The digital world is wild, weird and occasionally wonderful, but it can often feel like you're the only adult left in a land ruled by memes, emojis and videos of dancing cats.

First up, let's talk about the big news: Australia's social media ban. Picture this: you're at the kitchen table, trying to remember if you've already packed lunch for tomorrow, when your kid asks, 'Can I have a TikTok account? *Everyone's* got one!' You glance at the news and the headline reads: 'Australia Bans Social Media for Under Sixteens'. Suddenly, you're not just the parent; you're the enforcer of a modern digital law, the gatekeeper of the social feed, the last line of defence between your child and the endless scroll.

It might sound dramatic, but this new social media ban, aimed at protecting Aussie kids, is a game changer. A world first! As of now, Instagram, Snapchat, TikTok and their digital cousins are officially off-limits for our kids. The intention? To give them time to grow up in the real world before the algorithms force them to do it prematurely in the digital world.

But before you panic (or pop the champagne), let's take a collective breath. The good news is the social media ban puts parents, carers and teachers on the same page. We now have the Australian government in our corner; they can be the bad guys. 'Sorry, son, but it's illegal until you're sixteen.' We don't have to feel guilty for depriving our little sweethearts of their daily dopamine hit. It's the government's fault!

INTRODUCTION

This book is here to illuminate, educate and, occasionally, inject a little dad humour into the journey ahead. Because parenting through a digital revolution shouldn't mean you lose your sanity or any more sleep. We're here to help you navigate not only the ban, but device use in all its many forms.

Why this book? Why now? Devices are everywhere. They beep, they buzz, they beckon. For many kids, screens are as natural as breathing. But as the lines between real and virtual worlds blur, the stakes have never been higher for parents. Throw in a nationwide social media ban, and you've got a recipe for confusion, debate, misinformation and, let's face it, a few dinner table arguments.

Think of this book as your toolkit, your road map, your emergency snack stash for those days when device battles feel endless. It's here to help you. We will discuss what the social media ban really means for your family. How to set healthy, realistic boundaries with devices in a world that never stops buzzing. How to navigate tricky conversations with kids who 'just want to fit in'. Why finding a balance between screen time and green time (remember grass? It still exists!) is important for us all. And most importantly, why boundaries around device use will help *everyone* thrive in the 21st century.

There's a reason the phrase 'digital natives' was invented. It's not because our kids are any different to us, it's because they are growing up in a world where asking 'What's your

Wi-Fi password?' is easier than saying 'Hello'. Devices aren't going anywhere, and neither is the endless parade of apps promising to educate, entertain and socialise our kids.

But with great power (hello, AI) comes great responsibility . . . and a few headaches. What's the difference between healthy curiosity and a digital addiction? Is YouTube safe, educational, or just a rabbit hole of slime videos? And now, with the social media ban, how do you keep your kids connected to their friends while keeping their online lives safe?

First things first. The ban isn't intended to 'ruin childhood' or make you the family villain, though you might feel that way some days. It's meant to hit pause on kids' social media lives until they're a bit older. Old enough to handle the twists and turns of digital drama, privacy pitfalls and the ever-present lure of likes and influencers.

Will it stop every child from setting up a social media account? Of course not. Kids are clever and loopholes will be found. But the ban gives parents and carers a valuable tool. We now have a clear, national boundary to lean on. 'It's the law' is a lot easier to enforce than 'Because I said so'. Think of it as backup in your ongoing negotiations.

If you're worried your child will suddenly become a hermit without Instagram or TikTok, take heart. Despite the big tech companies' rhetoric, there is actually nothing *social* about social media (except for the name!). Social media platforms are all about advertising. Either advertising a product, service, event, or advertising yourself. The more 'friends' on social media, the fewer friends in real life. Kids are creative, social creatures when given the opportunity. They'll find ways to connect, whether it's through real-life meet-ups, group texts, or, gasp, picking up the phone for an actual conversation.

This could be a golden opportunity to teach your child about real friendships, empathy and the joy of being present. Imagine board games, bike rides, jumping in puddles and backyard adventures. These aren't relics of the past. With a little encouragement, they can become part of your family's present-day reality.

Parenting is hard enough and there is no manual. Now there's the added complication of online life, big tech companies, influencers and all manner of nefarious players vying for our kids' attention. No one wants to become the digital police. But no one wants their kid to become another digital zombie. The nice thing is that these changes put the responsibility on the social media companies to enforce the new rules. That's one thing we can stop panicking about.

It's important to remember that no one gets it right all the time. Not you, not your neighbour, not the expert on breakfast TV. There will be days when the screens win and that's okay. What matters is the conversation, the awareness and the willingness to keep trying.

It's also perfectly normal to feel overwhelmed. Tech changes fast. Policies shift. Our goal is to provide you with a trusted source of evidence-based, objective and independent information so you can deal with the overwhelm.

We'll take you on a journey into how we arrived at this point and, more importantly, how we can move forward so that our kids develop the skills they'll need in the future. Together we can create a world where they'll feel more connected, more resilient, more empathic and more in control of their mental and physical health.

So, what can you expect as you flip through these pages? We will:

- Explain the new social media rules and what they mean for your kids.
- Highlight the myths that are often touted and why they don't hold water.
- Break down the effects of screens on the development of the brain.
- Describe how and why some apps can be addictive.
- Explore the important skills kids need to develop to thrive.
- Unpack ideas for tech-free family fun and how to build real-world connections.

We'll explore the pitfalls of device use, like the increase in ADHD and autism diagnoses, but we'll also talk about the joys of discovering a new family game night. Most importantly, we want you to realise you are not alone in this. All around Australia, parents are wrestling with device dilemmas, negotiating with their kids, and wondering if anyone else's child has dropped the iPad in the toilet. Together, we can help our children grow into thoughtful, resilient and digitally savvy citizens. And who knows, maybe we'll even rediscover a little wonder ourselves along the way.

CHAPTER 1

The big beautiful ban!

As an Aussie parent in today's fast-changing world, it's natural to feel a little overwhelmed by all the talk of technology. You've probably heard about the new social media ban for kids under sixteen and are wondering what it means for your family. Why are these changes happening now? Do they really matter? Is there any risk in letting your ten-year-old have a Snapchat or YouTube account? Could these changes affect your child's education or friendships? If you're feeling confused about what's best for your children or why governments are making these new rules, you're not alone.

In the early 1800s, many people feared that novels could negatively influence young people. The Reverend Samuel

Miller warned in 1803 that 'no one was ever an extensive and habitual reader of novels ... without suffering both intellectual and moral injury'.[1] Similarly, the Reverend Enos Hitchcock lamented that 'the free access which many young people have to romances, novels, and plays has poisoned the mind and corrupted the morals of many a promising youth'.[2] Printed stories, then the closest parallels to today's immersive media, were viewed as potential threats to childhood innocence and development.

Looking back, these ideas seem almost comical. Imagine catching your little one having a sneaky read behind your back. Most of us struggle to cajole our kids into reading anything at all, yet we know books support their development in language, empathy and imagination. Still, even though we would give our left arm to have our kids reading regularly, some novels *are* inappropriate for certain ages and parents and teachers need to consider this.

Today we're a long way from the 1800s and the landscape is vastly more complex. Children now have access not only to books but also to a digital world that offers a constant flow of videos, messages and images coming at them at unprecedented speed and volume. The rapid pace and diversity of online content presents big challenges for parents trying to stay informed. While some online material is engaging, educational and beneficial, a lot is simply not suitable for kids.

But without the deliberate gatekeeping traditionally exercised with books, it's easily accessible.

That's why it's so important for us, as parents, to pause and think about what our children are experiencing online. The stories, images and messages they absorb don't just affect their schoolwork; they shape how they see themselves, how they relate to others, and even how well they pay attention or manage their emotions. In the past, we trusted caring adults to guide a child's reading and learning. Now, it's often algorithms with no empathy, context or understanding of our children's developmental needs that decide what pops up on their screens. Just as earlier generations learned to choose the right books at the right time, we must develop the same wisdom and vigilance for the digital age. The medium has changed, but the responsibility has not.

One reason for the new social media restrictions is pretty simple: we already limit kids' access to things like smoking, alcohol and gambling, because we know they're addictive and can be harmful. Young people just aren't ready to manage the risks associated with those activities. Social media is no different; it's designed to be addictive and it's been proven to affect a child's mental health and their developing brain. So, just as we protect our kids from other things they aren't ready for, it makes sense to put boundaries around social media too.

Some people say that kids need social media to learn how to be good 'digital citizens', but the truth is that many of us learned how to use these platforms as adults, without needing years of practice as children (although, there are a lot of adults behaving poorly online). We teach our kids about the dangers of alcohol and gambling and we wait until they're mature enough before letting them make their own choices. Social media, with all its potential pitfalls, is the same.

There's also been some confusion about whether the new rules will stop kids from learning online, especially from platforms like YouTube or TikTok. The reality is that the restrictions are about personal accounts for kids, not about blocking access to useful videos. Teachers can still show educational content and students can watch most videos without signing in. The big difference is that tech companies won't be able to collect personal data and target kids with addictive features or advertising. Such data has been a core driver of the business model for many online platforms. The change will not affect education despite the tech companies' rhetoric suggesting otherwise.

And what about socialising? While it's true that kids like to chat and connect, it's important to remember that social media platforms are designed for advertising, not for true social connection. Tristan Harris, co-founder of the Center for Humane Technology, worked for Facebook in the early days.

Tristan came up with a new button that, when clicked, sent a message to all your friends who were nearby and happy to meet up.[3] Facebook executives quickly removed the button because they realised it would facilitate *real-life* socialising. And when that happened, they knew people wouldn't be on their devices. Have no doubt that these apps are designed to keep kids scrolling, *not* to help them build real friendships.

Finally, some families worry that social media is important for young people from minority backgrounds, including the LGBTQIA+ community. While online spaces can offer support and information for individuals from minority groups, they are *four times* more likely to be harmed, bullied, trolled and experience negative mental health issues after spending time on social media.[4]

Unlike the 1800s – or even twenty years ago – the challenges today are far more complex. The sheer scale, speed and variety of digital content means that the boundaries of 'what is appropriate' are blurred. Too often, parents and educators are playing catch-up. While some digital material is wonderfully educational and uplifting, a lot of what kids consume online is simply inappropriate.

There's a ton of confusing stuff out there about the social media ban and it's no wonder parents are feeling lost. Even the Australian eSafety Commissioner changed its tune, going from being against the ban to supporting it, despite no changes in the evidence. Technology is big business, especially when it comes to kids. So how do we, as parents, make choices about what tech our kids use when there's so much money involved? It's important for us to be picky about where we get our advice. Ideally, we want experts who aren't tied to tech companies and who base their advice on what's best for our kids.

Some of the conflicts are obvious. YouTube and TikTok spend loads of money on ads highlighting the 'good' aspects of their platforms for kids and education, hoping to sway public opinion. But what's more worrying is that some groups running wellness programs in our schools, like URSTRONG and PROJECT ROCKIT, receive money from companies like Snapchat.[5] These programs insist they can be impartial and put kids first, but when big tech companies are pouring in cash, it's fair to ask questions about whose interests are really being served.

Some tech company owners don't let their own kids use much tech at all. Many send their children to Waldorf (or Steiner) schools, which keep screens out of the classroom, especially in the early years. In fact, at most Waldorf schools, primary students don't use tech at all; it's only introduced in the later years, and very intentionally. Families are encouraged, even expected, to limit screen time at home so kids grow up with consistent, healthy boundaries. Why? Because these parents and educators have seen the downsides of too much tech. They know that the next big idea or breakthrough isn't going to come from a kid who's a champion at video games or selfies, but from someone who's curious, creative and great at working with others. These are skills that come from playing sports, reading books, climbing trees, learning music, getting grubby and spending time with friends. Not from being glued to a device.

Dr Mark visits Aussie high schools all the time. He says that when he asks Year 7 students if they have a close friend they can talk to, almost all say yes, but by Year 12, only about 5 per cent do. Just five out of a hundred high-school seniors feel they have someone they trust. It's not just his experience – research is showing that school loneliness is out of control.[6]

As humans, we need to spend time with real people we trust. Hanging out with friends actually does more for our brains than anything else. It can help us live longer, fight off dementia, improve our mental health and even protect our hearts.[7] We're at our best when we're with our people, not doom-scrolling on social media.

The sad thing is, even when we're together, a lot of people stare at their phone, not each other. Social media is a funny term because most teens have tons of 'friends' online, but very few real ones. If we keep letting tech take over our social lives, important areas of our brains will become less functional. We need to act now if we want our kids to grow into healthy, happy adults.

Back in the 1950s, sneaky media companies started using 'subliminal advertising'. It was banned very quickly because it manipulated people's behaviour without them knowing. Today, social media does something similar but on a much bigger scale. Think notifications, likes, recommendations, and so on. All designed to keep us hooked. TikTok, for example, uses different algorithms in China than in Western countries to target kids in different ways. According to some experts, platforms like TikTok can shape what we believe and how we act, all while collecting a mountain of data about us.[8]

Parenting in the digital age isn't easy, but you're not alone. The world has changed, but our responsibility to protect and support our children hasn't. By staying curious, setting healthy boundaries and talking openly with our kids, we'll help them grow into resilient, thoughtful adults online and, more importantly, in the real world.

That's why the new social media ban is such a big deal. It's the first of its kind and way overdue. Is it perfect? No, but it's a step in the right direction. There will be stumbles, but that's just part of being human.

PRACTICAL TIPS TO HELP YOU NAVIGATE THE CHANGES

1. Frame the ban as *protection*, not *punishment*

Emphasise the ban's intent: safeguarding mental health, reducing exposure to harmful content and kerbing addictive design features like doom-scrolling.

Use analogies kids understand, like seatbelts or age limits for driving, to explain why some rules exist for safety.

2. Boost digital literacy

Treat this as a window to build your child's tech resilience.

Encourage critical thinking about online content, algorithms and digital footprints.

3. Have open, ongoing conversations

Talk about FOMO, peer pressure and the emotional pull of social media.

Validate their feelings while guiding them towards healthier habits.

Share stories and your own experiences with social media.

4. Offer alternatives for connection

Help kids find other ways to stay socially connected like group chats via messaging apps (for example, WhatsApp or Messenger Kids, which aren't banned) or in-person hangouts.

Encourage hobbies, sports or creative outlets that build identity and community offline.

5. Use parental controls and tech tools

Explore apps or built-in device settings to manage screen time and app access.

Keep devices in shared spaces and set tech-free times (for example, during meals or before bed).

Most importantly, know that platforms, not parents, will be held accountable for enforcing the ban. There are no penalties for families if kids bypass the restrictions.

A WAKEUP CALL FOR US ALL

If we are honest with ourselves, we know that the new rules on social media are not just about protecting children. They are also a reminder for us as adults to pause and take a good look at our own habits. If governments are stepping in because they recognise the risks to our kids' wellbeing, then surely those same risks apply to us too. Staring at our screens for seven hours a day, which is the average in Australia for an adult, is not good for anyone!

As the Italian physician and educator Maria Montessori wrote, we should always model the behaviour we hope to see in the children we care for.[9] It would be unfair to demand restrictions from our children if we are not willing to follow those restrictions ourselves. Children are born with a powerful sense of justice and can spot a double standard in an instant. If we say, 'These rules are for you, not for me' or the old classic 'Do as I say, not as I do', we risk losing their trust. Boundaries only carry meaning when they are shared. If we want our kids to respect them, then we must respect them too.

We're not expecting you to delete all of your socials and YouTube channels! This conversation we're having is not about perfection; it's about honesty and reflection. As adults we know how easy it is to slip into endless scrolling or constant checking. If we find it hard to manage our time online, then imagine what it must feel like for a child whose brain is still developing. The neuroscientist Vilayanur Ramachandran once said, 'Mirror neurons will do for psychology what DNA did for biology.'[10] These remarkable cells in the brain are the reason children so naturally copy the people they love and trust. What they see in us – our actions, our habits, the way we connect – becomes the blueprint for how they choose to live.

This is why the way we talk about rules matters. It is not enough to simply ban or restrict something. Rules imposed without explanation can feel unfair and arbitrary. But when we take the time to explain the reasoning behind them, children can recognise their value. Rational conversations create understanding, and understanding builds trust. When we speak openly about the risks of social media, about how addictive design works, about how time online can affect mood and sleep, children begin to see that these rules are not punishments. They are protections. Even children from a very young age can understand this concept if we explain it appropriately.

Of course, kids don't always like restrictions! They will push back. They will complain. But they will also notice when we follow the same boundaries ourselves. They will see that the rules are fair. And because of those mirror neurons, they will begin to internalise the rhythms of life that balance digital connection with human connection because we modelled them.

Marshall McLuhan, the Canadian philosopher who spent his life exploring how media and technology shape us, once said, 'We become what we behold. We shape our tools, and thereafter our tools shape us.'[11] Those words feel more relevant today than ever before. Social media platforms may present themselves as impartial tools, offering us connection and access to information, but they are far from neutral. They are designed with a single aim: to capture our attention and hold it for as long as possible. The real moment of power comes when we recognise this truth and then choose how we allow these tools to enter our lives. When we place boundaries around them, they lose their grip and their power is weakened. It is in this act of conscious choice that we reclaim the ability to shape our own lives and, more importantly, the lives of our families.

There's something exciting about what comes next. When we step back from our devices, even just a little, we begin to rediscover the world that has always been waiting beyond our screens. The laughter of a child sharing a story without the interruption of a beep or a ping. The rhythm of a walk in the fresh air without earbuds restricting the sounds of nature. The spark of a conversation that flows freely without a quick selfie or WhatsApp message interrupting it. These are not small things. They are the moments that give us energy, meaning and health – and we need them back.

As the writer and poet Mary Oliver once said, 'Pay attention. Be astonished. Tell about it.'[12] Her words remind us that the real future of our homes and schools will not be won by more apps and screens, but by reclaiming our time, focus and attention.

Once realised and then adopted, this is where wellbeing begins. Research shows again and again that too much screen time, especially when it takes the place of real human connection, is linked to anxiety, loneliness and depression. Dr Jean Twenge, an American psychologist and researcher who has studied generational shifts in behaviour for decades has shown that the more time kids and teens spend looking at screens, the more likely they are to show symptoms of anxiety and depression.[13] If this is true for teenagers, then it is true for adults as well. The same boundaries that protect our children can protect us too.

Australia's social media ban is not only a policy for the under-sixteens. It is a wakeup call for us all. It asks us to pause and look closely at how we spend our time, and to ask whether those choices reflect the lives we truly want to live. It challenges families and schools to create rules that apply to everyone, not just to some. And it reminds us that real health and happiness are not found in the endless scroll, but in the depth of our relationships, the freedom of time spent outdoors, and the richness of face-to-face connection.

This book is not about guilt. It's about opportunity. Every shared boundary, every conversation that makes sense, every moment we reclaim from the digital pull is a step towards a healthier life for us all. If we can take a lesson from the new rules and guidelines written for children and apply them to ourselves, then we will not only be protecting the next generation, we will also be healing and restoring our own.

In the end, technology is not going anywhere. But neither are the people we love. And when the choice is laid out for us, it's clear which one deserves more of our time.

THE BENEFITS OF THE SOCIAL MEDIA BAN FOR CHILDREN

Some might see the social media ban as a limitation, as if something is being taken away. But the opposite is true. By setting limits on how children engage online, we are giving them something far more valuable: the freedom to grow, the space to breathe, and the opportunity to develop the qualities they will carry into adulthood. This is not about cutting children off from the digital world. It is about creating the right conditions for them to build a healthy and balanced relationship with it.

One of the greatest gifts of the ban is time. Without the constant pull of scrolling and messaging, children are free to immerse themselves in the things that bring joy and meaning. Playing, reading, exploring outside, creating and daydreaming are not distractions from real life. They *are* real life. These moments build the foundations of imagination, resilience and confidence in a way that screens never can.

They also give children the time to build the skills of the future in a natural way, not inside a screen but by exploring and experimenting in the world around them, using all of their senses and not just their eyes fixed on a blue light. The Australian Institute of Family Studies reports that children aged four to five are already spending more than two hours per weekday in front of screens. By the time they are twelve to thirteen, this rises to more than three hours per weekday and nearly four hours on weekends, which adds up to around 30 per cent of their waking time.[14] Imagine what children could gain if even part of that time was given back to play, connection and discovery.

The ban also protects the deeper skills children will need for the future. When they are not caught up in likes and followers, they have time to focus on problem-solving, creativity, empathy and collaboration. These are the abilities that prepare them to lead, to innovate and to thrive. No algorithm can teach them what it feels like to comfort a friend, to climb a mountain, or to build something with their own two hands.

These moments will be etched into their minds for a lifetime, a constant reminder of how good it feels to be alive and active in the world with the people we love, instead of spending whole days recording hundreds of TikTok videos just to gain likes from followers they have never met and likely never will.

Most importantly, the ban gives children the chance to connect with the world in ways that feel genuine and alive. It draws them back to the natural environment, to friendships that grow beyond a screen, to the thrill of discovering something new. This kind of connection is not fleeting or shallow. It stays with them, shaping who they are and how they see their place in the world.

The social media ban is not about shutting doors. It is about opening the right ones at the right time. Social media will still be there when children are old enough to use it, but by then they will have already discovered how magical it feels to connect with other people, how to explore the world around them, to try new things, and to experience what it truly means to be human. When this happens, social media naturally takes a back seat, because our children will have developed the critical awareness to understand that their time is finite, and that no one has the right to take it away from them.

THOUGHT-PROVOKING STATS

Ninety-seven per cent of Australian teenagers use social media every day.
A Mission Australia survey of more than 17,000 young people aged fifteen to nineteen found that daily use of social media is almost universal, with 38 per cent spending three hours or more per day on these platforms.[15]

Seventy-four per cent of children aged ten to seventeen have encountered harmful online content.
Research by the eSafety Commissioner reveals that nearly three-quarters of Australian children aged ten to seventeen

have been exposed to harmful material, such as violence, misogyny or unhealthy diet promotion, and 63 per cent experienced this within the last twelve months.[16]

Hospitalisations for self-harm among teenage girls have increased by 70 per cent.

Data reported by the Royal Australian College of Psychiatrists shows that hospitalisations for intentional self-harm among young Australian women aged fifteen to nineteen surged by 70 per cent between 2008–09 and 2021–22, with social media identified as a significant contributing factor.[17]

These figures show *exactly* why the government has taken the bold step of banning social media for kids under sixteen. They point to a growing awareness of how these platforms shape not only our kids' development but also their mental health. With mental health issues on the rise, and with the understanding that the choices we make today will be reflected in the adults who walk our streets twenty years from now, this decision is not just about the present. The government's ban is about the future.

It is about asking what kind of citizens we want as the custodians of our country and of the wider world. When we recognise the scale of the problem, it becomes clear that the ban is not about restriction for its own sake. It is about creating the right conditions for healthier and more balanced childhoods.

WHAT CAN PARENTS DO?

1.   Letter writing night

Once a month, get together as a family with hot chocolate, candles and some quiet music. Each person writes a letter to someone they would like to make feel happy. It might be a grandparent, a teacher, a friend or even someone far away who inspires them. Every family member chooses their own recipient. This simple ritual builds gratitude, empathy and a sense of global connection. As the bishop Carl W. Buehner once said, 'People will forget what you said, people will forget what you did, but people will never forget how you made them feel.'[18] For children, it shows the power of words and reminds them that kindness travels across distance and time. When the letters are sealed and sent, the whole family feels the joy of brightening another person's day.

2.   Invite a friend for dinner

Once a week, give your teenager the chance to invite a friend from school to share your family meal. It does not need to be fancy, just another plate at the table. This act gives your child a sense of pride as they share their home and family with someone they care about. It shows their friends that they are welcomed and valued. As the theologian Desmond Tutu said, 'My humanity is bound up in yours, for we can only be human together.'[19] For children, these evenings build confidence, strengthen social skills and help them feel that they belong to something bigger than themselves. For parents, it opens a window into their child's world and nurtures trust.

3.   Work beside each other

Choose a time for the family to sit together and work side by side. Parents might answer emails, pay bills or fold laundry while children do homework or projects. In Montessori education, this is called 'parallel work'. It is a quiet form of companionship that communicates respect: your work is just as important as mine. The US political figure and former first lady Eleanor Roosevelt reminded us, 'Unless equality, freedom and mutual respect are present, no lasting human progress can be achieved.'[20] This practice models focus, patience and discipline in a way that children can observe and imitate. For families, it turns everyday tasks into moments of connection and shows that productivity can be shared and peaceful.

4.   Host a family movie night

Set aside one evening a week for everyone to curl up together on the sofa with blankets, popcorn and a film. Let each person have a say in choosing what to watch so that the tradition feels fair and fun. This time is not just about watching a screen, it is about being together. The small rituals of preparing snacks, voting on the movie and sharing reactions make it special. As the US TV host and author Fred Rogers once said, 'Connections are built on simple, everyday moments of showing up for one another.'[21] For children, a family movie night builds a sense of family tradition, teaches compromise and creates memories that will last long after the credits roll. These evenings remind us that when families connect through joy, those bonds grow stronger.

5. Read the same book together

Choose a book and let each family member read their chapters independently. At an agreed time, maybe in the car on the way to school or even when walking together at night, talk about what happened in the story, the choices the characters made and what you think might happen next. Mum and son might be reading one book while Dad and daughter are reading another, creating pairs who bond over the same journey. This practice turns reading into a family affair. It shows that learning is not just something for children but a lifelong experience that we all share. As the American journalist Mary Schmich wrote, 'Reading is a discount ticket to everywhere.'[22] For children, it builds comprehension, empathy and reflection while reminding the whole family that stories can connect us across ages.

THE BENEFITS FOR OUR CHILDREN

When we sit together for letter writing night, invite friends over to share a family meal, work quietly side by side, enjoy a weekly film together or regroup after reading, the effect goes far beyond the activity itself. These simple practices are not just replacements for social media, they are richer and more lasting experiences that give children a deep sense of belonging, inclusion and respect. They show that learning is lifelong and that connection grows strongest in the ordinary moments of family life. Over time, these habits shape the way children see themselves, the way they relate to others and the way they understand their place in the world.

Although some of these practices may feel unfamiliar at first, maybe even a little awkward, they soon take on a special meaning. What begins as something new becomes sacred not just for the children but for you as well. Children thrive on routine, and these small rituals reach far beyond education. They become memories etched in their minds for life, remembered as times of connection, belonging and love.

FIVE POSITIVE OUTCOMES WE CAN EXPECT

Richer attention and focus

When the noise of constant notifications is taken away, children rediscover the beauty of giving their full attention. Cooking a meal together, writing a thoughtful letter or sinking into a story are all invitations to concentrate deeply. These moments teach that focus is not a burden but a gift, and it becomes the foundation for success in learning, relationships and life.

Stronger emotional wellbeing

Shared routines such as a family film night or working quietly side by side promote laughter, comfort and stability. They give children healthy ways to manage feelings and to feel safe in uncertain times. A child who knows the joy of belonging and the comfort of being seen does not need to chase approval through likes. Instead, they carry within them a deep well of security and love.

Deeper connection to people and community

Inviting a friend over for dinner, reading alongside a parent or reconnecting with neighbours are small acts that remind children they are part of something bigger. These practices build teamwork, generosity and inclusion in ways that social media cannot. Real friendships, built face-to-face, become a network of trust and support that lasts long after a post is forgotten.

Expanded skills and creativity

Hands-on experiences, whether writing letters, discussing stories or creating small household projects, allow children to discover hidden abilities. These are not simply hobbies, they are stepping stones to resilience and confidence. Unlike the fleeting distraction of scrolling, these skills remain, building pride and joy in the act of making and doing.

A stronger sense of belonging

When parents give their time to children through simple routines like meals, conversations and shared traditions, children feel seen, heard and valued. They know they matter. This is the heartbeat of family life. It is within these ordinary moments that children learn they have a secure place in the world, surrounded by people who love them for who they are. This sense of belonging cannot be replicated by technology. It becomes the anchor they carry for life.

IN SUMMARY

The purpose of the social media ban is not to take something away, but to give something back. It is a chance to recover what matters most. What children gain is not simply less distraction, but the opportunity to grow up in the presence of deeper connection with themselves, with their families and with the world around them.

When families gather for meals, learn alongside one another, watch a film together on the sofa or walk beneath the stars, we are not just filling the empty spaces left by screens. We are building traditions that our children will carry into adulthood. We are planting memories that tell them, again and again, that they belong, that they are valued, and that they are loved.

This moment asks us to pause and reflect on what we as parents are modelling. It invites us to show our children that true joy comes from presence, not distraction, and that what lasts in life is not measured by followers or likes, but by the bonds we weave day by day.

By choosing to spend our time in ways that honour connection, we are giving our children more than just a childhood, we are offering them a foundation for lifelong wellbeing. They will remember the laughter, the shared meals, the stories and the quiet evenings. And once they have felt the strength of that belonging, it will guide them long after childhood has passed.

These reflections and activities may take up time, but it is time so well invested, not only in our children, but in ourselves. Human beings are a connected species, and shared moments of belonging are gifts that ripple far beyond the walls of our own homes. Everyone who is part of them benefits. From the boy who is welcomed to dinner at your table this week, to Uncle Pete who receives a letter from your family across the ocean in America; these acts of connection remind us all that we matter to one another.

CHAPTER 2

Our relationship . . . with our phone

Do your kids seem to *love* their phone? Do they always tend to have it within reach and take it everywhere they go? Do they often break off conversations to check it or respond to it, spend countless hours alone with it, and seem emotionally attached to it? Maybe this applies to you too. Have you ever thought about how truly bizarre it is to have such a close relationship with a device? Back in 1925, the Catholic Bishop Fulton J. Sheen said, 'Love people and use things, rather than love things and use people.'[1] We think he would be shocked at the current state of the world.

Never in history has a new technology been so overwhelmingly accessible. No matter your age, sex or nationality, most of us can get our hands on a smartphone. In little more than fifteen years it's gone viral. Who hasn't seen babies in prams, unable to yet walk or talk, staring at a tiny screen? Or teenagers at the beach playing on their smartphones and adults on a dinner date busily texting away? There are even photos of tribesmen in Papua New Guinea, complete with headdress, face paint and spears, taking selfies. No matter where you go or what people are doing, they are absorbed in a tiny screen. Is there any other technology that we have embraced so obsessively?

Let's take a trip down memory lane and look at some major tech breakthroughs. First up, the printing press in the 15th century. It was like the original Kindle, but with a few catches: hardly anyone could read and it was super expensive. For years, it was mainly used to reproduce the Bible. It took over *five hundred years* before books became as common as pink cowboy hats at a Taylor Swift concert.

Next, we have the aeroplane, invented by the Wright brothers in 1903. Flying was so pricey that only the uber-rich could afford it when commercial airlines took off in 1909. It wasn't until the 1980s that flying became more common in wealthier countries, and even today, many people around the world have never been on a plane.

Now let's talk about televisions. The first mechanical TVs popped up in the 1800s and the first electrical TV was invented in 1927. When television broadcasting officially began in Australia in 1956, for the Melbourne Olympics, less than 5 per cent of households had one. It wasn't until the late 1960s that Australian homes embraced the idiot box. Nowadays, most homes have at least one TV, but it's still nothing compared to the smartphone explosion.

The smartphone is the Usain Bolt of technology. In just over fifteen years, it has spread around the world like wildfire. From tribesmen in Papua New Guinea to babies who can't even walk, everyone has a smartphone. We've never seen anything like it!

Have you ever wondered why the smartphone became so ubiquitous in society so quickly? Why, in less than twenty years, our kids became digital zombies tethered to tiny screens? In the past, new technologies were out of reach for the average person. They were either not accessible due to the knowledge required, the high cost, or because there wasn't the underlying infrastructure. New tech like smartphones are cleverly designed to be easy to use, attractive and relatively affordable. They also use infrastructure that's already available. It usually takes time for technologies to become commonplace. The shift from 'new and peculiar' to 'desirable' and finally to common or 'essential' typically takes decades, if not centuries. But this did not occur with the smartphone.

Why is this important? Well, usually we have time to evaluate the pros and cons of a new technology on a smaller number of people – typically adults – before we allow kids access. This allows us to view the new technology from afar while a few wealthy groups experiment with its effectiveness and potential effects. We had none of that with the smart-phone. We went from zero to a thousand kilometres an hour virtually overnight. Instead of a small group of 'guinea pigs' testing it first, our kids have been given access to technology that we are only now realising has significant effects on their brain development and overall mental and physical health.

If everyone had a phone but only used it occasionally, that would be one thing. But the way we use smartphones is a whole other story. These little gadgets are now part of every activity. Did you know that more than 80 per cent of people keep their phone within arm's reach twenty-four hours a day?[2] That means when they go to the bathroom, when they go to bed, when they wake up in the middle of the night, when they are on a date, or even during intimate activities – you name it, the phone is there!

Our kids are growing up with a phone in their faces around the clock. If it's turned off or runs out of battery, it can cause great stress and anxiety. People have embraced this new technology so enthusiastically that 25 per cent of teens would rather lose their voice for a day than go without their phone. How do your kids react when they forget their phone? How often are they without their phone?

Another major difference with smartphones is that they are being used by people of all ages. In the past, new technologies were always first restricted to wealthy or powerful adults. Because of the initial cost, very few (if any) children or teenagers had access. If they did, it was under the strict supervision and control of an adult. For example, television, when it first appeared, and for several decades, was restricted to the living room of the family home. There was an adult around to supervise what the child was watching. There were many experiments done and discussions held over decades on what was and wasn't appropriate for kids and teens to watch. And government legislation and guidelines were published well before televisions appeared in young people's bedrooms. Not so for the smartphone.

In Australia, 37 per cent of kids under twelve and a whopping 91 per cent of teens aged fourteen to seventeen have their own smartphone.[3] Have you ever wondered what effect using a smartphone might have on their brains? I'm assuming, since you're reading this book, it's something you're interested in. Unfortunately, the early signs are that things might not be okay.

The developing brain is precious and our kids are spending so much time on their smartphones that their brain development is in danger. In Australia, kids between five and twelve spend over 4.5 hours per day on their devices, while teenagers spend over 7.5 hours outside school time on theirs. There are vital stages in brain development that occur from birth to twenty-five years of age, and for the brain to develop correctly, it needs certain experiences. Kids need to be doing 'real' things in the 'real' world. We have no idea what spending such large amounts of time on a device will do. We are currently conducting a worldwide, unprecedented experiment . . . with no control group!

How much time do your kids spend on their phone or a device each day? Three hours? Five hours? More? And what about you and your friends? What are we all doing on our phones for that long every day? We know that for most people, at least half of this time is spent on social media like Facebook, Instagram and TikTok. The latest research shows that the more time we spend on social media, the more likely we are to become anxious and depressed.[4] Our kids and, let's be honest, most of us adults are being wired up to be dependent on smartphones – and unwired from the real world.

Now, we don't want to sound like old grumps! We both use our smartphones too; they're useful a lot of the time. And Dr Mark has teens at home who also have smartphones. But we've also noticed the effect it has on us and the people around us. And we've looked at studies done all around the world to find out what the effect of social media, gaming and the like might be having on us. Unfortunately, it's not good. Thousands of scientific studies published in the past fifteen years show devices are having negative effects on us. Scientific studies have shown increased rates of anxiety, depression, social isolation, stress and suicide, combined with decreased intelligence, attentional control, empathy and resilience. Maybe it's time for a rethink?

What is your relationship like with your phone? What is your kids' relationship like with their phones? Do you, as a family, spend time together without a device present? Do you or your kids get anxious when your phone battery runs low? How many hours do you and your kids spend on your devices each day? Does anyone in your family love their phone more than the wonderful people around them? Let's explore the evidence together and see how we can get the benefits without the costs; how we can do digital differently.

And given this is getting a bit heavy, here's a dad joke for you. Why did the smartphone need glasses? Because it lost all its contacts!

MODELLING A HEALTHY RELATIONSHIP WITH TECHNOLOGY

Have you ever found yourself reaching for your phone without thinking? Perhaps you were waiting for the toast to pop, sitting in the car at school pick-up, or walking through the house, only to realise your hand had somehow found your pocket and your phone had found your face. These moments have become so routine that we barely notice them, but our children do. In fact, they notice *everything*.

One of the things we've observed time and time again is the power of modelling behaviour. Children are incredible observers. They study us with more intensity and detail than we often realise. They're not just listening to what we *say*, they're watching what we *do*. And when it comes to technology, what they see is shaping the way they'll live.

We live in a world that is more digitally connected than ever before, yet many of us feel increasingly disconnected in our day-to-day relationships. Technology and smartphones in particular have shifted how we interact with each other, how we spend our time and even how we parent. The shift has been fast, widespread and largely unexamined.

The arrival of smartphones didn't drift in slowly, it arrived like a tidal wave. In just over a decade, we've gone from phones that made calls to devices that manage every corner of our lives: calendars, photos, messages, meals, alarms, entertainment, banking and more. And along the way, a quiet but significant change occurred: our phones started competing for our attention in the very moments that matter most.

Studies now show that the average Australian spends 5.67 hours on their phone every day and checks their phone eight times an hour. That's about 125 times per day.[5] We unlock, swipe, check, respond, refresh. Non-stop. On the surface, these actions seem harmless, but cumulatively, they send a powerful message to our children: *this is what matters.*

More than 95 per cent of teenagers in Australia have access to a smartphone and 72 per cent of parents openly admit that their own habits are influencing those of their children.[6] This awareness is a powerful starting point, but awareness alone isn't enough. Change begins with reflection.

There's a well-known phrase in Montessori education: 'The child is both a hope and a promise for mankind. As the adult is the environment of the child, he must perfect himself to offer the child what is necessary.'[7] But it's not just the physical environment that matters, it's the emotional, social and behavioural environment too. In this case, we are the environment. We are the model.

From a neurological perspective, the science backs this up. A child's brain is not just passively developing, it is actively wiring itself in response to the world it encounters. Rich human connection, conversation, eye contact and unhurried play are all key ingredients for strong cognitive and emotional development. These experiences build empathy, critical thinking, creativity and resilience.

Too much screen time, especially in the absence of human connection, has been consistently linked to increased anxiety, loneliness and depression in children and adolescents. Dr Jean Twenge has studied this area extensively and writes, 'Teens who spend more time on screens are more likely to be unhappy, and those who spend more time on non-screen activities are more likely to be happy.'[8]

Children don't need us to be perfect, they need us to be present.

When they're telling us about their day and we're checking an email, they notice. When we stop a conversation mid-sentence to read a notification, they feel it. Over time, these small moments accumulate. They teach children that their voice comes second to a huge array of other, more pressing priorities. And unknowingly, we set the foundation for what they believe relationships look like.

Modelling a healthy relationship with technology doesn't mean abandoning our devices or pretending they don't have value. Technology is here to stay and it offers benefits, con-nection, creativity, access to information and convenience. But we must be the ones who demonstrate how to use it with intention.

This might mean charging phones outside the bedroom to protect sleep routines. It might mean putting devices away during mealtimes to create space for uninterrupted conversation. It might mean making a habit of walking to school without a device in hand; just you, your child and the world passing by.

Children do not need long lectures about screen-time limits. They need to *see* what balance looks like. They need to *feel* what connection looks like. They need to *experience* what it means to be heard, seen and prioritised in the presence of someone who *could* be distracted but chooses not to be.

As adults, we are constantly modelling behaviour for our children, whether we realise it or not. If we want them to grow into brave, kind and resilient individuals, then we must live those qualities ourselves. The same is true when it comes to our use of technology. If we hope to raise children who are focused, present and intentional, we must demonstrate those values in our own lives first.

In Montessori education, we often speak of the 'prepared adult', a calm, intentional presence who guides through example, not through force. In the modern world, preparing ourselves means reflecting on the role technology plays in our lives and asking whether that role is aligned with the kind of future we want for our children.

This is not about guilt, it's about opportunity. Every small shift we make, every phone turned face down, every conversation held with full attention, every choice to prioritise human connection helps our children learn to do the same.

Ultimately, technology isn't going anywhere. But neither is the power of presence. And our children need both, but they need presence more.

THE BENEFITS OF A HEALTHY TECH RELATIONSHIP

When it comes to technology, it's easy to focus on the negatives: too much screen time, the distractions of social media and the potential for digital overload. But the truth is, technology isn't inherently harmful. In fact, when we use it with intention and purpose, it can be a powerful tool for connection, creativity and learning. We are not suggesting banning screens altogether, but rather helping children (and ourselves) build a thoughtful, balanced relationship with them.

Technology brings people together. It keeps us connected to family and friends who may live on the other side of the world. It opens up a vast universe of knowledge that children can explore at their own pace, feeding their curiosity and independence. And for those creative minds, it becomes a canvas, whether they're composing music, animating a story or capturing their own voice in a short film. When guided well, these experiences can nurture confidence and self-expression.

Technology also plays a practical role in our everyday lives. Devices can help manage family routines, remind us of appointments and even support children in building organisational skills. When used mindfully, technology can act as a supportive tool in a busy household; not a distraction, but an assistant. The key lies in how we model this balance ourselves. By showing children that screens can serve our lives, not take over them, we guide them towards a healthy, lifelong relationship with the digital world.

The key is balance, and this is something that children learn not through rules alone, but through what they see and experience at home.

THOUGHT-PROVOKING STATS

Australians spend nearly seventeen years of their lives on their phones.

The average Australian spends 5.5 hours a day on their smartphone, which equates to 16.6 years over a lifetime, assuming phone use begins at age ten.[9]

Ninety-one per cent of Australian teenagers own a smartphone.

A 2023 survey found that 91 per cent of young people aged fourteen to seventeen owned a smartphone, highlighting the pervasive presence of digital devices in teenagers' lives.[10]

Parental screen time may negatively affect children's development.

A study by the University of Wollongong found that excessive use of digital devices by parents can disrupt parent–child interactions, potentially leading to poorer cognitive and social development in children under five.[11]

These figures paint a clear picture: our relationship with our devices doesn't just shape our day-to-day lives, it shapes our children's future.

WHAT CAN PARENTS DO?

1.   Model the behaviour you wish to see

Children pay close attention to how adults behave. They might not always listen to what we say, but they never miss what we do. The habits we live each day, whether it's reading, exercising, eating well or showing kindness are the habits our children are most likely to adopt. If we want them to value books over

screens, movement over sitting, or conversation over distraction, we must show them through our own choices. The writer James Baldwin once said, 'Children have never been very good at listening to their elders, but they have never failed to imitate them.'[12] By modelling the attitudes and behaviours we hope to see, we give our children a living example to follow.

2. Establish tech-free zones and times

In Montessori environments, the physical space is intentionally designed to invite focus, engagement and independence. The same principle can be applied at home. Try designating certain areas, like the dining room or bedrooms, as tech-free zones. This helps protect time and space for conversation, reflection and calm. Setting aside tech-free times can also support family bonding. Meals, walks or one evening a week without screens can become moments to reconnect. As the writer Helen Keller once said, 'The best and most beautiful things in the world cannot be seen or even touched, they must be felt with the heart.'[13]

3. Practise mindful phone usage

One of the most powerful things we can model for our children is mindfulness. Before picking up your phone, ask yourself, 'Is this the best use of my time right now?' Often, we reach for devices to fill a quiet space or avoid discomfort, but these are the very moments where growth and connection can occur. Mihaly Csikszentmihalyi, the psychologist who introduced the concept of 'flow', wrote, 'Control of consciousness determines the quality of life.'[14] In other words, how we choose to spend our attention shapes the lives we lead. When children see us using technology for the right reasons and only when necessary, they are more likely to do the same.

4. Prioritise face-to-face interaction (eye time)

Personal interaction is essential for healthy emotional development. It's through face-to-face conversations that children learn empathy, read social cues and build trust. Make time for activities that involve shared attention, playing games, telling stories, gardening or learning something new together. These moments don't need to be grand. What matters is the quality of your presence. As author Jim Rohn observed, 'One of the greatest gifts you can give to anyone is the gift of attention.'[15]

5. Promote family projects

One powerful way to reduce screen time is to introduce family projects that involve creativity, teamwork and purpose. Whether it's planning a picnic, building a bird house or creating a family recipe book, these shared experiences anchor children in the real world. Why not try a regular 'digital detox day' where everyone agrees to switch off for a while? Let the children help choose the activities for the day. These rituals not only strengthen relationships but also remind us of the joy that can be found away from screens.

THE BENEFITS FOR OUR CHILDREN

When we consistently prioritise the simple, foundational practices of family life by being truly present in a conversation, creating deliberate tech-free zones where connection can flourish, modelling our own mindfulness, choosing face-to-face moments, and embarking on meaningful family projects together, the effects reach far beyond a single peaceful mealtime or an evening without arguments over the laptop.

Each of these small and somewhat insignificant but conscious choices is a vote for the kind of family we want to be. They are quiet, powerful statements that communicate what we truly value, not with our words, but with our most precious resource: our attention.

And without noticing, over time these repeated actions seep into the very bedrock of our children's understanding of the world around them. They begin to internalise these priorities, not as a set of rules they must follow, but as the natural rhythm of what it is to live in a world where we are truly connected. The value we place on listening, creating and simply being together is absorbed into their character, quietly shaping the way they think, how they behave in moments of stress or joy, and the depth with which they connect with others for the rest of their lives.

And with that, here are five positive outcomes we can expect to see, both now and in the years to come.

Improved attention span

Children who are given regular opportunities to focus without the interruption of screens develop deeper concentration. You might notice them sticking with a puzzle longer, becoming more absorbed in a book or taking greater care in completing tasks. These moments of uninterrupted focus are the foundations for all future learning.

Stronger emotional regulation

By modelling calm, thoughtful behaviour and giving children time and space to process their emotions without digital distractions, we help them develop self-regulation skills. Over time, this means fewer meltdowns, greater patience and an improved ability to manage disappointment or frustration.

Greater sense of connection

Children who experience regular, device-free conversations, especially with the adults they trust most, develop stronger bonds and a deeper sense of belonging. These connections provide emotional security and are often what children return to during times of stress or change.

Increased independence, creativity and brain growth

When children are given less access to mindless entertainment – games and apps that simply distract rather than add value – and more time for unstructured play, something powerful occurs. Boredom emerges, and rather than being a *problem*, it becomes a *gateway*. In that stillness, children start to build, create, role-play, draw and solve problems entirely on their own. In Montessori education, we call this kind of deep, purposeful exploration 'big work'. Big work not only fosters imagination and independence but also strengthens the brain itself, building synaptic connections that support lasting learning, focus and emotional resilience.

A healthier, purpose-driven relationship with technology

When children grow up seeing technology used to solve problems, create meaningful work or connect with purpose, they begin to view it as a tool, not a constant companion. They come to understand that screens have their place, but they are not essential for every moment of life. This shift in mindset nurtures a sense of control, rather than dependency, and encourages children to turn to technology when it adds value, not just to fill space. Over time, this intentional approach helps them build a more balanced and thoughtful relationship with the digital world.

IN SUMMARY

Our goal isn't to remove technology from our children's lives, but to illuminate the path through it. In a world where digital noise is constant, our quiet modelling speaks volumes. It's not the rules we impose, but the choices we make in front of them, every time we look up from a screen, choose presence over distraction, or make space for connection, that shape their habits and their values.

By creating tech-free sanctuaries, embracing meaningful pauses, and treating technology as a tool rather than a lifeline, we offer our children something far more lasting than digital literacy; we offer wisdom. And within that wisdom lies a deeper message: that they are worthy of our time, our attention and our presence.

In modelling a conscious relationship with technology, we're not just teaching them about the role it plays, we're reminding them that life is meant to be felt, not filtered. Not lived through seven hours a day, totalling sixteen years behind a glowing screen, but through awe, wonder, adventure and human connection. And once they feel that difference, they carry it forward. They become the gatekeepers of a more mindful, meaningful way of living.

CHAPTER 3

Use it or lose it

Did you know that our brain is like a superhero, constantly changing and adapting every day? Every time we learn something new, make a memory or have an experience, our brain gets a little upgrade. It's like having a superpower! The human brain is the most complex thing on Earth, with 86 billion neurons and over 100 trillion connections. That's more connections than there are stars in the Milky Way! And don't forget the glial cells, which are like the brain's personal assistants, outnumbering neurons ten to one. This amazing network lets us see, touch, feel, hear, taste, love, hate, think, learn, remember, dream, walk, talk and do all the other cool stuff we do every day. It's mind-blowing!

One of the coolest things about the brain is its ability to change itself. You've probably heard about brain plasticity in the media, where people recover from accidents or strokes by retraining their brains. But guess what? Our brains are *always* changing, even without any drama. Everything we do, say, hear, read, see and experience reshapes our brain. It's how we learn and remember things from moment to moment and day to day. Your child's brain today is different from the brain they had yesterday, and it'll be different again tomorrow based on what they do today. Talk about a brain makeover!

Think of brain plasticity like a garden. When we learn something new, it's like planting a seed. With each new experience, we're watering and nurturing that seed, helping it grow into a strong, healthy plant. If we neglect the garden, the plants wither away, but if we tend to it regularly, it flourishes and becomes a beautiful, vibrant space. So keep planting those seeds and watch your brain garden thrive! And of course, this is even more important for our children.

Ever thought about becoming a taxi or Uber driver? These days, all you need is a licence, a car and a smartphone. But back in the day, drivers had to rely on paper maps or their memory. In London, taxi drivers still take pride in navigating the streets without a device or map. They have to pass a super tough test, learning the entire layout of London and proving they can get from one place to another without peeking at a map. It takes years of study to pass this test. In 2002, Professor Eleanor Maguire and her team discovered that London taxi drivers have a larger posterior hippocampus (the brain region involved in navigation). It's like having a built-in GPS![1]

The London taxi driver experiment showed that even adult brains can change. Learning something new can significantly reshape our brains, no matter our age. But there's a downside to this amazing ability – if we don't use certain skills, we can lose them. Just like our muscles, our brains need regular exercise. If we don't use it, we lose it!

A more recent example of how our brains constantly change arose out of a study on reading by Professor Stanislas Dehaene and his colleagues in France. They investigated an area of the brain that represents words. The interesting thing about this area is that it is usually on the left side. On the same spot on the right side is the area that codes for faces. They were interested in what this area might be used for in people who are illiterate. They did brain scans with a group of people in Brazil and found that those who had not learned to read had two areas dedicated to coding faces. After they learned to read, they rescanned their brains and found that they now had a word area on the left side (just like us). Learning to read changed their brains.[2]

The concept of 'use it or lose it' has been demonstrated in many different contexts. When children are severely deprived, their brains develop abnormally both in structure and in function. To put this another way, their brains look very different to a child who has grown up without any deprivation. The same thing happens at the other end of the lifespan. It used to be common practice for nursing home residents to have very limited stimulation. They would spend long hours either alone or sitting in a common area watching TV. They had little or no control over what they did during the day or what meals they ate. By simply giving nursing home residents things to do to stimulate their brains, they live longer. But not only do they live longer, they live *better*. The rate of brain diseases such as Alzheimer's and Parkinson's also drops significantly. If they are using their brains, they don't lose their minds.

So the 'use it or lose it' concept has spawned an industry of its own. There are now many companies that organise outings for the elderly or activities in nursing homes. A recent study showed learning a musical instrument post-retirement reduces your likelihood of getting dementia. This is fantastic for those reaching the later stages of life. Anything that can reduce the likelihood of brain disease and make our last years more enjoyable is a win.

But maybe you're thinking, 'How does this relate to my kids? They're not old and ready to retire. They're young and fit and need to check what's happening on TikTok.' Here's how it's relevant: kids need to develop a whole bunch of important abilities during their childhood and teenage years in order to maintain those abilities as they get older. With so many kids reliant on their smartphones, they are getting limited experiences and choices and this is affecting their brains.

How many things do kids do on a smartphone rather than in their head? When was the last time they navigated their way to a friend's house without using a smartphone? When was the last time they did a maths calculation in their head rather than using a smartphone calculator? When was the last time they sat and chatted with a friend without looking at a smartphone? And when was the last time they sat quietly and just imagined rather than checking a smartphone? Now think about all the other things humans used to do with our brains that we now do on our devices. Those are all the abilities that we are losing.

The problem with devices like smartphones is that they limit our experience and learning. We don't have to navigate, remember, calculate, consider, imagine or interact with the world and others anymore. And like the nursing home residents of yesteryear, if we don't use these abilities, we lose them.

When Dr Mark mentioned this to a group of students, one of them said, 'But I have my smartphone, so I won't need these abilities.' Another student then jumped in and said, 'Yeah and AI is great and even better tech will come soon so we will never need them.' We felt like dropping to our knees and crying.

We are at a real tipping point. Smartphones are being seen as a replacement for our brains. But we need our brains to live, to breathe, to walk and run, to think, to love, to understand and to be our own unique selves.

When a kid is waiting at the bus stop or sitting in a café, do they ever just contemplate the world? Do they ever just daydream? Does anybody daydream anymore? The ability to daydream or imagine may be a uniquely human experience.

Our rise to become the apex species is due partly to our ability to imagine. Discoveries and innovations happen because of this incredible ability. But like all abilities, it needs to be exercised and practised. Who is going to come up with the 'next big thing' if we are all on our devices and never exercise this critical ability? We wonder what impact this will have on our innovation ... that's a scary thought, isn't it? What we do know is it won't be a smartphone that imagines the next great leap forward.

Maybe you think we're sensationalising this. Perhaps, but let's consider some of the results that are coming out in the research. Professor Evelyn Law and her colleagues have shown that infants who are given access to a device develop abnormal brain activity and perform poorer academically when they eventually attend school compared with those who are not given devices.[3] And work by Professor John Hutton and his colleagues has shown that white matter tracts in the brain are altered by the amount of time children spend on screens. These tracts can be thought of as the highways in our brain that allow the different areas to communicate. The more time children spend on devices, the more abnormal these tracts are, creating structural changes in the brain.[4] So we already have evidence that the structure of the brain changes with device use.

How might that affect brain function? Well, we also have evidence of abnormal brain function as a result of screen use. The younger a person has access to a device like a smartphone or tablet, the more likely they are to have attention deficits. Smartphones and other devices are designed to capture attention. The bright colours, the movement and the sounds are very difficult to ignore. All these constant attention-grabbing stimuli means that when we are on our devices, we don't get the opportunity to train our attention to stay in one place on one task. We need to practise the ability to maintain attention and to ignore irrelevant stuff. Otherwise, we end up slaves to our environment. Flipping from one task to another. Flipping from one beep, or flash, or buzz. Devices don't allow us to practise this important ability and so we never develop it. And for those of us who grew up without smartphones? Guess what, we are losing it!

This is a major issue for us all. Some countries are installing traffic lights in the footpath because pedestrians won't look up from their phones! Even when their lives are in danger, they cannot shift their focus. The number of accidents caused by people absorbed by their mobile phones when they're walking or crossing the road is staggering. Our inability to attend to anything but our phones is literally maiming and killing us. It is crazy to think that this is where we have ended up. So just take a minute to consider: could your kids be missing out on important abilities because of their reliance on a smartphone?

Our over-reliance on devices is changing how we pay attention, remember and interact. Even basic skills like safely crossing the street are being compromised. We must ask ourselves if we're sacrificing our children's mental abilities for convenience.

It's not all bad news though. The flip side to this discussion is that our brains are incredibly adaptable. Neuroplasticity means that if you and your kids start using your brains, they'll adapt and change just like your muscles. So blow the dust off those dumbbells, take the washing off the exercise bike, put all the devices away and start working out your body and your brain.

By the way, why did the smartphone go to school? Because it wanted to be a smart phone! Maybe we would prefer for our digital natives to be smart kids instead.

ARTIFICIAL INTELLIGENCE AND YOUR CHILD

There was a time, not so long ago, when a child's world was shaped almost entirely by human interaction. Teachers led classrooms. Parents read stories at bedtime. Friends whispered secrets in the playground. Every experience and every lesson was passed down through voices, faces, hands and heartbeats. But in recent years, a new presence has entered this space, quietly, seamlessly and often unnoticed: artificial intelligence (AI).

AI doesn't knock at the door. It simply appears, embedded in voice assistants, streaming platforms, digital learning tools and even the toys our children play with. It finishes our sentences in text messages. It recommends what we should watch next. It subtly learns our preferences and uses them to influence what we buy, read or listen to. For adults, this might seem like a welcome layer of convenience. But for children, whose brains are still growing, who are learning what it means to be human, the presence of AI introduces questions we must not ignore.

As educators who advocate for a healthy use of technology at home and at school, we've long believed that technology itself isn't the problem. It's our relationship with it that matters most. And AI, while remarkable in many ways, can condition us and our children to become passive recipients rather than active participants in life. It suggests, recommends, interrupts and completes. And over time, if we're not careful, it can begin to think *for* us.

The research reflects this concern. According to the World Economic Forum, more than 80 per cent of people now use AI-powered tools daily, often without even realising it.[5] These tools include predictive text, curated news feeds, virtual assistants and learning platforms – technology that adapts and personalises content in real time. For children, this can create the illusion that the world revolves around their preferences, that every question has an immediate answer and that every desire should be met instantly.

But childhood isn't about answers, it's about exploration. It's about curiosity, uncertainty and learning to tolerate the unknown. AI, for all its brilliance, can interfere with that process. It can train the mind to expect shortcuts, validations and immediate results. In doing so, it may hinder the very qualities we're trying to nurture: patience, critical thinking and independent decision-making.

Children don't need to understand how an algorithm works to feel its effects. They may not realise that their YouTube suggestions are powered by machine learning, but they do notice how one video quickly leads to five more. They experience the draw of endless entertainment and the ease of instant gratification. And more importantly, they quietly absorb what they observe in us: the constant checking, the quick google for every question, the subtle dependence on devices. Over time, they begin to mirror those habits, not because they understand the technology, but because they're learning from the example we set.

This is where our role as parents becomes crucial. Our job is not to shield children from the digital world but to guide them through it. We must help them build a relationship with technology that is conscious and balanced, not reactive or unquestioned. And this guidance starts with us. We need to look at how we interact with AI ourselves. Do we allow it to shape our decisions without reflection? Do we turn to it as a default? Are we modelling curiosity or convenience?

One of the most important things we can help our children understand is that AI is just a tool. It's not a teacher, a parent or a friend. It can help us find answers, offer suggestions, or make things easier, but it will never replace human wisdom, empathy or imagination. If we want our children to grow up using technology responsibly, we need to show them how to use it with care and thought.

That might mean asking questions when AI gives a suggestion, like, 'Why do you think it recommended that?' or 'What's another way we could find out?' It could be as simple as pausing a voice assistant during dinner or choosing to play a board game together instead of watching another movie picked by an algorithm. These small moments might seem minor, but they speak volumes about the kind of choices we value. And when these moments are modelled and openly discussed, our children begin to think for themselves, rather than letting the machines think for them.

One recent study from UNICEF and the Berkman Klein Center at Harvard University suggests that children need *supportive dialogue* around AI, not warnings or restrictions. They need open conversations about what AI is, how it works and how to think critically about its role in their lives. The study found that children who engaged in these types of conversations with adults were better able to spot manipulation and retain a sense of agency in digital environments.[6]

And that's our ultimate goal: agency. To raise children who can think for themselves, question what they are shown and choose when to switch off and re-engage with the world around them.

AI is not going anywhere. But neither is the need for children to climb trees, build cubbyhouses, get bored, write stories, ask wild questions and create things that algorithms can't predict. These are the spaces where true learning occurs.

The Montessori perspective is rooted in balance. We don't fear the future, but we do observe it carefully. We ask, 'Is this helping the child grow in independence, resilience and empathy?' If not, it's our responsibility to adjust course, not through panic, but through presence.

We don't need to fear artificial intelligence, but we do need to remain alert to its influence. Our children are not passive recipients of technology; they are active meaning-makers, constantly learning from their surroundings. The way we use AI, how we speak about it, question it and set limits around it will quietly teach our kids how to do the same.

This generation will grow up with machines that can recommend, predict and perform. But no machine can replace a parent's wisdom, a teacher's patience or a child's imagination. These are human gifts and they remain at the heart of everything that matters.

Let's keep those gifts at the centre of our homes, our classrooms and our decisions. Because while AI may shape the future, it is our values, our presence and our example that will shape our children.

THE BENEFITS OF A BALANCED RELATIONSHIP WITH AI

When used with intention, AI can offer real value to families and children. But the key lies in balance. These tools are at their best when they support, not replace, human interaction, creativity and critical thinking. Some AI-powered learning platforms can be genuinely helpful, especially when they adapt to a child's pace and style of learning. For children who struggle with certain concepts, this kind of tailored support can build confidence and engagement. It's not a replacement for a teacher's wisdom or a parent's encouragement, but it can be a useful companion on the learning journey.

AI is also showing up in ways that offer practical peace of mind. Apps and wearables, when used responsibly, can alert parents if a child wanders too far or enters an unsafe environment. It's an added layer of care, but only when it's used with trust, not surveillance. Equally important is what AI can teach us about itself. When children begin to understand how algorithms work, how recommendations are made, or why their feed looks the way it does, they start to develop real digital literacy. Instead of passively consuming content, they learn to ask questions. 'Why did it suggest that?' 'Who made this?' These moments spark awareness and build the kind of critical-thinking skills that will serve them for life.

Perhaps most exciting of all, AI can be a launch pad for curiosity. Used in the right way, it invites conversations about fairness, ethics, justice and the way the world works. These are big questions. And when we explore them side by side with our children, we're not just guiding them through the digital world, we're inviting them to shape it with thoughtfulness, purpose and care.

THOUGHT-PROVOKING STATS

The average American interacts with AI more than two hundred times a day.

According to a 2022 survey by Reviews.org, 76.5 per cent of people use AI within ten minutes of waking up and 58 per cent say they couldn't go a full week without it.[7]

Ninety-five per cent of American teenagers have access to AI through smartphones, speakers and online platforms.

A Pew Research Center study found that most teenagers interact with AI-based tools regularly, including smart assistants, facial recognition tools and social media algorithms.[8]

Seventy-seven per cent of parents are concerned that AI presents new internet safety risks for their kids.

A national survey by the New York Society for the Prevention of Cruelty to Children found that most parents worry AI is making it harder to protect their children online.[9]

These stats make one thing clear: AI isn't just something children are aware of, it's already shaping the way they learn, play and connect. That's why it's more important than ever that we help them understand it. Not with fear or restrictions, but with calm guidance, open conversations and real-world examples of how to use it wisely.

WHAT CAN PARENTS DO?

To help children strengthen their minds instead of outsourcing their thinking to AI, we need to invite them to participate in activities that challenge their memory, reasoning, attention and imagination. Here are five practical ways to do just that.

1. Build a mental map walk

Leave the phone at home and go for a walk with your child. Before you head out, study a printed map together or sketch a simple route. Choose landmarks like an old tree, a bright red postbox or a corner shop and see if you can find your way using only your memory. Ask questions along the way, like, 'Which street did we just pass?' or 'How will we get back?' This kind of activity strengthens your child's spatial memory and develops the hippocampus, just like the London taxi drivers. As Albert Einstein said, 'Look deep into nature, and then you will understand everything better.'[10] Let this be a reminder that the world around us is still the best classroom we've got.

2. Set a weekly 'memory challenge'

Choose one thing to memorise each week; a short shopping list, a poem, a phone number, five important dates, a speech or a song. Write it down, practise it aloud, even sing it together and check in later to see what's remembered. This small act reawakens the part of the brain responsible for recall, sequencing and focus. 'Tell me and I forget, teach me and I may remember, involve me and I learn,' said Benjamin Franklin.[11] When we involve our children in actively using their minds, we send the message that their brain is not just a backup drive, it's the main engine.

3. Solve problems without a screen

When a question pops up, 'What's the capital of Peru?' or 'How do you fix a dripping tap?', pause. Don't reach for your phone. Instead, wonder aloud. Think it through together or check a book. Maybe you're wrong, maybe you're right. Try to solve it together because that moment of uncertainty is gold. It teaches children that not knowing is the beginning of learning. It's in the figuring-out that growth happens.

4. Invent something from nothing

Set up a small box of scrap materials – string, paper, tape, bottle caps, paperclips and cardboard – and challenge your child to invent something. A new game, a musical instrument, a contraption for their bedroom. There's no right or wrong. This is play with purpose. It builds creative confidence, problem-solving and the joy of experimentation. And as the

geographer and author O. Fred Donaldson said, 'Children learn as they play. Most importantly, in play children learn how to learn.'[12] That's what invention really is: play with the brain switched on.

5. Start a collection together

Ask your child to choose something they'd love to collect – feathers, buttons, shells, badges or stamps – and start building the collection together. Let them organise, label and display the items with care. The simple act of collecting builds patience, attention to detail and pride in personal interests. As Maria Montessori put it, 'The hands are the instruments of man's intelligence.'[13] Through collecting, children are refining their sense of order, storytelling and focus, using their hands and hearts to understand the world around them.

THE BENEFITS FOR OUR CHILDREN

When we create healthy boundaries with AI and embed meaningful, human-centred practices into our daily lives, the effect on children is transformative. These become more than just habits, but an exposure to the reason why we are using *anything* to assist us.

Sharpened critical thinking

When children aren't constantly being told what to watch, play or choose next by a machine, they start to take back control of their decisions. They begin to wonder, 'Why am I seeing this?' or 'Is this really helpful for me right now?' It's in these small questions that independent thinking takes root. Rather than accepting everything at face value, they begin to pause, reflect and explore other possibilities. In a world where so much is curated for us, teaching our children to think for themselves is one of the most powerful gifts we can offer.

Stronger self-regulation

Resilience isn't built in comfort, it's built in the moments when things *don't* go to plan. When we step back and give children the chance to solve problems on their own, without offering instant fixes or quick digital distractions, they begin to discover what they're capable of. They learn that it's okay to feel stuck and that trying again is part of the process. Over time, this builds patience, perseverance and the ability to manage emotions. These aren't just useful skills; they're the foundation of lifelong confidence.

Deeper connection with family

Some of the richest memories we create with our children come from the simplest moments: sitting around the table, walking without a phone, laughing over a board game. These shared experiences become emotional anchors, quietly telling our children, 'You matter. I'm here.' In a world filled with online comparison and noise, these moments of genuine connection act as a buffer. They remind children that they are seen, heard and loved, and that real connection can't be downloaded or streamed.

Greater curiosity and creativity

When we make space for boredom – real, quiet, open-ended boredom – something amazing happens: children start to invent. Without a screen feeding them entertainment, they begin to follow their own questions, explore their own ideas and make things up from scratch. They write stories, build dens and create imaginary worlds, all from within. This is where true creativity comes alive. It's not driven by algorithms or likes, but by inner motivation and wonder. And that kind of curiosity stays with them for life.

A healthier relationship with AI

When children see AI used with intention, whether it's helping us find a recipe, organise a calendar, or explore a big question, they learn that it's a tool, not a necessity. They stop expecting it to entertain, comfort or think for them. Instead, they begin to use it when it adds value, and step away when it doesn't. This balanced approach protects them from overuse and helps them feel in charge of their digital world, not controlled by it. That sense of agency is what turns tech from a distraction into something empowering.

IN SUMMARY

AI isn't going anywhere and we wouldn't want that, but neither is our responsibility to guide children through an AI-powered world with wisdom, intention and heart. As parents and educators, we hold a quiet kind of power, not in the rules we enforce, but in the way we live. In the rhythms we create, the boundaries we protect and the choices we model, we shape how our children come to see technology: not as something to surrender to completely, but as something to use with care and purpose.

When we choose presence over distraction, conversation over convenience and curiosity over control, we're doing more than just parenting in a digital age; we're planting the seeds of discernment, empathy and agency. And in doing so, we give children something far greater than any device can offer: the ability to know themselves, to connect with others and to shape the world with intention, on screen and far beyond it.

CHAPTER 4

Attention for sale

Do you find it hard to concentrate? Do you get distracted easily? Do you check your phone constantly? And what about your kids? Does homework time feel like a cage fight? Do you feel like you need to chain them to the chair? If you answered yes to these questions, you're not alone. And finding answers isn't easy. Nor is it completely within our control. Tech companies design smartphones and apps to grab our attention. The more they succeed, the harder it is to resist. They wear down our attention span, making it tough to stay focused. But what *is* attention and why does it matter so much?

Attention is like our brain's filter. The world is a busy place and getting busier. Our brain can only handle so much at once. Attention helps us decide what's important. It lets us focus on what we want to see, hear or think and blocks out the rest so that we are not interrupted. Right now, you are hopefully absorbed in this book and the words on the page! You're probably not noticing the noises around you or the feeling of the chair on your back and bum (except now you probably are because I directed your attention to them!). Our attention is always filtering out certain information so we can focus on what's most relevant or important.

Phones have always been good at capturing our attention. Remember the old-fashioned ones that were wired up to the wall? When they rang, we knew someone wanted our attention. And that annoyingly loud sound was impossible to ignore. In those days, the phones had only one purpose: to make and receive phone calls. And they were tethered to a wall. Nowadays our phones do everything, from sending emails to monitoring our heart rate. They're always with us, pulling us away from what we're trying to concentrate on.

In the days before smartphones, the system was analogue. Only one person could try to grab our attention at any point in time. With smartphones, there is no limit to how many people can interrupt our peace, 24/7. We get emails and notifications from our workmates, our kids' coaches and teachers, our family, our friends. It's endless. We get likes on social media and updates from apps. We've gone from a situation where we could be interrupted by only one person at a time to a situation where we can (and often are) interrupted by literally thousands (and most of those people we have never met).

And guess what? You're probably interrupting thousands of people too without even realising it. Every time you update your Instagram or comment on TikTok, your 'friends' are notified. How many people are you linked to on social media? How many times do you like, comment or update each week? Each action potentially interrupts *thousands* of people. In the past we thought about it before we interrupted someone. Picking up a phone to ring someone is a behaviour that is the result of a thought process. Now we aren't intentionally interrupting people – that would be rude, wouldn't it? Now tech companies use our input to interrupt thousands of people daily.

Consider your kids. They are living in a world where they are being *constantly* interrupted. Their brains are constantly jumping from one notification to another. A relentless interruption that is pulling them away from life.

So how do smartphones and apps grab our attention? They still use that old-fashioned ring (or a fancy ringtone you set up). Noise is a great attention-grabber. Our ancestors needed to detect sounds quickly for survival. It's easy to imagine how useful this would have been. If something was approaching from behind or in the dark, you would want a quick detection system. Is it a snake, a lion, or a neanderthal with a club? Noises attract our attention and the louder or more obnoxious that noise, the harder it is to filter out. Old phones did this well, but modern phones have more tricks up their sleeves.

Touch or vibration is another attention-grabbing technique that modern phones use. Our sense of touch evolved as a great survival mechanism. Being able to feel a spider or snake crawling across our leg was important for our ancestors. So too feeling our way around in a dark cave before we had control of fire. Today our smartphones vibrate to attract our attention.

Using vibration has been so successful that it has resulted in a new disorder. It is called phantom vibration syndrome and while not yet officially recognised by the medical profession, it is causing some concern. Phantom vibration syndrome is an hallucination that occurs when somebody believes their smartphone is ringing (vibrating) when, in fact, it isn't. According to Professor Michelle Drouin and her colleagues, 89 per cent of undergraduate students in the US have experienced phantom buzz syndrome.[1] And not just young adults! A school principal told us they get phantom buzzes on their wrist at night after they take off their smartwatch. What a great demonstration of how attuned we are to vibration (and how annoying!). Have you ever felt a vibration on your leg, only to find your phone didn't actually buzz? I bet your kids have had the same experience.

Movement is another attention-grabber. When we get a message, the screen lights up. Our visual system is wired to detect movement, which was – and still is – crucial for survival. But now each notification distracts us from the present and pulls us back to our phones.

These methods are incredibly effective. A 2019 survey found that about half the population constantly checks their smartphones and feels distracted from important tasks.[2] Most people check their phones every four minutes. Think about that. Fifteen times an hour your attention is diverted to your phone. Why do we do that? What are the effects on our activities, mood and health?

It's frustrating to think about how much time these tech companies take from us. But it's not just our time. What about our kids? They haven't yet developed their ability to direct their attention. The important areas of their brain that should be practising focusing and concentrating are in a frenzied state when they're on their devices.

There is a link between smartphone use and Attention Deficit Hyperactive Disorder (ADHD). ADHD is a condition that affects many aspects of a person's life, including their performance at school and later work, and health and well-being. Professor Chaelin Ra and her colleagues have proven that the more time teens spend on their devices, the greater the risk of developing ADHD. These teenagers did not have any symptoms of ADHD before the research started and developed the disorder during the two-year study. Younger children given smartphones are also at higher risk of developing ADHD. The tech companies' practices are affecting our health and wellbeing and increasing attention disorders in our children.[3]

In this age of constant distractions, it's getting harder and harder to stay focused. Imagine making coffee without a filter. You'd end up with undrinkable sludge. Well, attention is like that filter, helping us focus on what really matters. But guess what? Our devices are like sneaky little sludge-makers, removing our filter and making it tough to concentrate.

Have you ever had a day where you had to concentrate hard for long hours? Most days, right? By the end, you felt drained and just want to veg out. Do nothing and eat some junk food in front of the TV. That's because you've used up your attention capacity. You need time, sleep or exercise to reset it.

It is not just concentrating hard for long hours that uses up your attention capacity but also how many times you *switch* your attention. You have probably heard about multitasking. Many people claim they can do lots of things at once. Actually, we humans are incapable of multitasking. What we do is task *switching*. We concentrate on one task and then switch to another and back again. And this switching takes extra attention resources (your ability to concentrate). You use up your attention resources more quickly if you are switching between two tasks rather than concentrating on one.

Because your devices are so good at capturing your attention, they're effectively causing you to switch your attention from your current task to your devices. Every time they do this, you lose focus on what you are doing and your attention capacity is eroded. Think about how many times your phone dings, beeps or vibrates each day. Each of those attention-capturing events switches your attention and affects your ability to think deeply.

Why are smartphones designed to capture our attention? If it is so bad for us and our kids to be distracted all the time, why are tech companies using these techniques? It comes down to money. You've probably heard the quote, 'If something is free, you're the product.' If you're not paying, they're making money another way. A lot of apps are either free or very cheap. These companies make their money through selling advertising. As the old saying goes, 'There's no such thing as a free lunch.' Apps are all about selling your attention and time to advertisers. Do you want you and your kids to be a slave to tech companies, using up your precious time? It's time to take back control!

When Dr Mark talks to students about the importance of

attention, he often shows them a photo of Times Square in New York City. It's a great example of marketing overload with huge, animated billboards everywhere you look. Companies pay big bucks to grab our attention. Times Square is a fascinating place to visit but overwhelming to live in. Your smartphone is a mini Times Square in your pocket. Imagine trying to be productive in Times Square – you'd be constantly distracted.

Thankfully, it is not too late to teach our kids that in the grand circus of life, they're the ringmaster of their attention, so keep those distractions in check and enjoy the show!

HOW TO FOCUS ON THE RIGHT THINGS

What if our children are not struggling to focus because they're lazy or distracted, but because they're doing *exactly* what the modern world has trained them to do?

Look around and you'll see it everywhere. Adults scrolling while pushing prams. Teenagers toggling between multiple apps. Toddlers tapping on screens with a speed that's almost unsettling. This is the culture our children are growing up in and they are absorbing it in ways we often don't see until the consequences begin to emerge.

We live in a time when attention has become a commodity. Big tech platforms and entertainment giants compete for it ruthlessly, because attention brings engagement and engagement brings profit. The clever systems behind our screens are designed not to support concentration but to break it, offering instant gratification, endless novelty and just enough dopamine to keep us coming back for more.

For children, whose brains are still developing, this is especially concerning. The ability to focus, to stay with a thought or a task, is foundational. It underpins creativity, self-regulation, deep thinking, empathy and resilience. When children lose this skill, it doesn't just affect their ability to finish homework, it changes how they experience the world.

But it isn't a hopeless situation. Children can absolutely learn to focus, but they need help. Not through punishment or restriction, but through deliberate, thoughtful guidance.

Research shows that attention is not a fixed trait. It's a practice. The more we use it, the stronger it becomes. But the reverse is also true. When attention is constantly interrupted, it weakens over time. A 2021 study from the University of California found that giving children even just twenty minutes a day of uninterrupted focus time – no screens, no multitasking – can dramatically improve their overall concentration within a few weeks.[4]

So how do we rebuild that capacity in a world working so hard to erode it?

It begins with the environment. Children thrive in spaces

that support calm, sustained activity. That doesn't mean silence or strict routines, it means pockets of time where the mind can wander, concentrate and return to a task without being pulled away. It could be a corner for drawing. A table for building. A patch of sunlight on the floor for reading.

It also means creating rhythms that value depth over speed. Our culture often rewards the fast finish and the flashy product, but children need permission to take their time, to linger, to repeat, to revisit and to refine.

And of course it all begins with the adults around them. Focus is not something we can demand from our kids while modelling distraction ourselves. If we are constantly checking our phones, jumping between emails, or half-listening while scrolling, we are sending a clear message: sustained attention isn't necessary. And children pick up on that message, whether we want them to or not.

Reclaiming focus in family life doesn't require rigid schedules or digital detoxes. It starts with small acts of presence. Putting the phone down when your child walks into the room. Finishing one task before starting the next. Watching your child play without offering commentary or correction. These moments are quiet, but they're powerful.

We also need to offer children *something worth focusing on*. When we create rich, engaging, real-world experiences – making bread, building dens, planting seeds, solving a tricky problem, for example – kids lean in. And when they do, they begin to remember what it feels like to lose track of time in the best possible way.

Boredom plays a role here too. In fact, it's vital and definitely not something to be fixed. Boredom is a necessary pause in the rhythm of life, a gap where the imagination starts to stretch. It's often in those quiet, unfilled moments that children create their most original ideas.

Of course, screens will remain part of their world. This chapter isn't a call to throw out every device. Rather, it's an invitation to restore balance. To remember that while technology offers stimulation, it rarely offers depth. And depth is where growth happens.

Children deserve the chance to fall in love with slowness. With getting stuck and trying again. With finishing something not for praise or points, but for the quiet satisfaction of having done it well.

Genuine concentration can't be drilled into a child, it must be lived. When we give children the freedom to disappear into something that truly matters to them, they carry that feeling like a compass and will keep seeking it out. Our task is to continue clearing the path so they can return to that place, again and again.

We don't need flawless homes, airtight schedules or picture-perfect children. What matters is that we stand guard over the fragile gift of focused attention, before a noisy world persuades them it can't exist.

THE BENEFITS OF LIMITING ACCESS TO TECHNOLOGY

When we gently limit the presence of digital devices in a child's daily life, we open up space for something far more powerful: connection, creativity and calm. The effects are noticeable almost straight away. With fewer distractions, children start to settle. They become more present, more engaged and more in tune with the world around them. And over time, those small changes begin to build into something lasting.

Focus and concentration are two of the first things to improve. Without the constant ping of notifications or the pull of passive entertainment, children find it easier to dive deep into a task. They're able to sit with a challenge, stay with it and see it through. That kind of cognitive stamina isn't just good for schoolwork, it's essential for life. The ability to think deeply, to hold a thought, to finish what you started; that's where true learning begins.

Of course, at first, it can feel like more work for parents. Children might seem louder, messier, more restless. But isn't that what childhood is supposed to look like? Movement, laughter, noise, curiosity; it's all part of the process. And soon, that chaotic energy begins to shift into something even more powerful: independence. That's the sweet spot. When children start directing their own play, solving problems, making things and navigating the world with confidence, you'll know it was worth it.

With less stimulation bombarding the brain, creativity starts to flow more freely. Children begin to use their imagination again, to build, to write, to draw, to pretend. It's in those moments of so-called 'boredom' that ideas emerge. That's where problem-solving starts and innovation is born. And with fewer screens soaking up the day, children naturally move more. They run, they climb, they play. Not only does this support their physical health, but it also lifts their mood, helps them sleep better and even sharpens their thinking. More movement, more connection, more creativity – that's the kind of growth no app can provide.

THOUGHT-PROVOKING STATS

Singaporeans use their smartphones an average of 5.3 hours a day.

This includes messaging, taking photos, reading the news and staying connected.[5]

One hundred per cent of Singaporeans aged fifteen to twenty-four use smartphones, compared to just 60 per cent of those over seventy-five.
This age disparity shows how deeply embedded these habits are in younger generations.[6]

Ninety-two per cent of Singaporean parents are concerned about the effects of device use on their children's health.
Addiction to devices (90 per cent) and access to inappropriate content (88 per cent) are also top concerns.[7]

These numbers don't just show us how much we're using devices, they reveal the shape of childhood as it's being quietly redrawn. Behind every percentage is a child learning how to connect, how to cope, how to grow. And in a world this noisy, it's never been more important to make sure they can still hear the sound of their own thoughts.

WHAT CAN PARENTS DO?

1. Introduce family activities and games
To bring focus back to real connection, try introducing screen-free family rituals: board games, collaborative cooking, craft sessions or storytelling, for example. These

moments build more than just fun, they form the foundation of childhood memories and secure relationships. As the philosopher George Santayana reflected, 'The family is one of nature's masterpieces.'[8]

2. Embrace outdoor activities

Nature has a way of quietening the mind and resetting the soul. Hiking, gardening, picnicking, or simply walking together through a park creates shared experiences that nourish both body and spirit. The naturalist John Muir captured it perfectly, 'In every walk with nature one receives far more than he seeks.'[9]

3. Introduce 'digital detox jars'

Sometimes, all we need is a gentle nudge away from the screen and back into the world. A 'digital detox jar', filled with slips suggesting activities like painting, dancing, journalling or crafting, offers just that. It's a playful invitation to presence. Anne Lamott reminds us that, 'Almost everything will work again if you unplug it for a few minutes, including you.'[10]

4. Cultivate non-digital interests

Encouraging children to pursue hands-on hobbies like baking, gardening, music or art gives them an outlet for creativity and self-expression. Hobbies offer a natural sense

of flow and achievement, helping children build identity and resilience. 'A hobby a day keeps the doldrums away,' wrote Pulitzer Prize–winning poet Phyllis McGinley, and it still holds true.[11]

5. Model the behaviour you wish to see

Children learn presence by witnessing it. If we want them to value calm, attention and balance, they must see it in action. That means setting down our phones, being fully present and embracing real-time connection. The poet Ralph Waldo Emerson once said, 'What you do speaks so loudly that I cannot hear what you say.'[12] The world teaches children many things; our actions should teach them what truly matters.

THE BENEFITS FOR OUR CHILDREN

When we help children reclaim their attention, we give them tools that serve them far beyond childhood. These aren't just daily wins, they're life skills.

Greater mental clarity and focus

When children learn to tune out the noise and sit with a single task, something powerful happens; they begin to think more clearly. With fewer interruptions, their minds settle and they're able to follow ideas through to the end. It's not just about better schoolwork, it's about the satisfaction of finishing what they started and knowing their thoughts have space to grow.

Increased sense of purpose

Scrolling rarely asks anything of us. But when children shift their time towards activities that require effort – building something, helping someone, learning a skill – they start to feel a spark. That spark becomes identity. It's how children begin to recognise their strengths and feel the quiet pride of doing something that matters.

Stronger emotional resilience

The more time children spend in real-world connection – laughing with a friend, solving a problem, navigating a tough moment – the more emotionally equipped they become. Without the constant comparison and noise of the online world, their mood steadies and their inner voice grows stronger. It's here they learn to ride the waves, not be pulled under by them.

More meaningful relationships

Presence is a form of love. When children show up fully in a conversation, without distraction, they begin to understand what real connection feels like. They learn how to read a face, hold a pause, feel someone else's joy or sadness. These aren't just social skills, they're the building blocks of belonging.

Healthier long-term habits

Learning to unplug isn't just about screen time, it's about learning to be at ease in your own company. When children are given the chance to be bored, to wait, or to wonder, they begin to build a kind of quiet strength. These early habits shape how they'll relate to technology for the rest of their lives, not as something to escape into, but something to use with intention.

IN SUMMARY

One of the biggest challenges facing our kids today isn't just screen time, it's what they're missing in its place. In a world that's constantly buzzing, pinging and fighting for their attention, moments of stillness, wonder and deep focus are slipping through the cracks.

We're not going to shut the digital world out, and we don't need to. But we *can* bring balance. We can give our children a taste of something richer: the joy of making an object with their hands, the thrill of being lost in a story, the grounding peace of a walk through nature, or the warmth of a conversation that isn't cut short by a notification.

Ultimately, attention isn't just about *concentration*, it's about *connection*. It's how children come to understand themselves, the world and their place in it.

So the goal isn't perfection. It's presence. And if we can create even a few sacred spaces where our kids can feel what it's like to be truly immersed in something meaningful, they'll come back to that feeling again and again for the rest of their lives.

That's the spark we're protecting. And it's worth everything.

CHAPTER 5

Getting dumber

Do you have trouble remembering facts or solving maths problems? Do you often sit at your desk struggling with an issue or challenge? Do you find it hard to remember people's names or even what you did yesterday? Are you worried about your kids' ability to remember their maths times tables or even to put the dishes in the sink? Or, maybe like many people, you haven't even noticed these things because you're so distracted by your device!

In 2016, Dr Mark started a new neuroscience course for first year undergraduate students. He spent a lot of time working with his colleagues to design the course and have it at the right level of complexity based on his experiences of teaching in the early 2000s. But he was shocked when they rolled out the new course. It was way too hard for most of the students. He talked to colleagues from other departments and other universities and the reply he got was basically, 'Yes, that would be right, the standard has dropped consistently over the past ten years. We've had to make course work easier to ensure the same percentage of students pass.' Each year, the first year cohort is less able to deal with complex information and organise their assignments. In response, courses are getting easier! But why?

Intelligence is an unwieldy beast. It is not easy to pin down what we mean by intelligence and it is even harder to measure. One common way is using a measure of general intelligence called the Intelligence Quotient (IQ). You've probably heard of it. You may have even had your kids tested. It's basically a number that is calculated after an intelligence test has been completed. There are a lot of issues with IQ testing including the fact that it is highly correlated with wealth and opportunity, but that's a discussion for another time. An IQ test, although a bit of a blunt instrument, is quite good at encompassing what most of us think is 'intelligence'.

Since we first started measuring IQ over a hundred years ago, the population has slowly become more intelligent. This slow increase in intelligence, year after year, is called the Flynn effect, and it's seen each generation get smarter than the previous generation.[1] There are multiple reasons for this including greater access to education, better nutrition and improved healthcare. But what is really interesting – and just a little bit worrying – is that in the last decade, the Flynn effect has *reversed*. The average IQ of people in many countries, including Norway, Denmark, Britain, the Netherlands, Sweden, Finland and yes, Australia, is now declining!

The reversal of the Flynn effect has been blamed on several different factors. One suggestion is that a decrease in nutrition with the increase in fast food and other processed goods may be affecting recent generations. Another is a change in how schools teach. There has been a shift in many countries away from explicit teaching to more student-centred learning. It has also been argued that better-educated women tend to have fewer children, which could affect the overall population's IQ. It is always difficult to pinpoint the exact cause of population changes, but what we do know is that there is a decline.

Studies into the decline in IQ reveal a specific pattern of results. The areas most affected are verbal comprehension, perceptual reasoning and perceptual organisation. As it is not IQ overall that's declining, but rather specific domains, it cannot be due to more general factors. For example, the fact that educated women have fewer children cannot explain the downturn unless you argue that only women with this pattern of intelligence are having fewer children. It also rules out nutritional causes as there is no reason to suspect that nutrition would have a specific effect on only some domains of IQ. Finally, the changes in teaching and school systems would predict a general shift rather than a specific pattern.

So what might account for this pattern of decline? Let's have a look at each of the affected abilities in turn. Verbal comprehension is a measure of a person's capacity to understand what is spoken to them. Phones were originally used to call people and (dare we say it!) chat with someone. Today, texting, messaging and emailing are far more prevalent than calling, especially among our kids. People don't chat like they used to. How many times have you seen a group of teens standing around together all staring at their phones? Chatting while waiting for a bus or an elevator, while with friends at the park or while at the beach is a dying art. As we saw in Chapter 3, if you don't use it, you lose it. So maybe it's a lack of practice that's leading to the decline in verbal comprehension.

The next two abilities that are affected are perceptual reasoning and perceptual organisation. Broadly speaking, these are the ability to process things visually, organise them, interpret them and solve problems. These are very important skills that require us to be in the world and solve problems that we see. If our kids are constantly staring at their 2D screens, when are they in the real 3D world solving problems? It's plausible that the new devices are the culprit when it comes to our decline in intelligence. Especially when you factor in the number of hours our kids are on their devices at school as well.

Just having a smartphone close to you has a detrimental effect on your intelligence! Professor Adrian Ward and his colleagues had participants place their phone either face down on the desk beside them, in their pocket or in another room.[2] The phones were set to silent so they wouldn't capture their attention. They found just having a device close affected their intelligence and working memory.

Dr Mark regularly presents the research on the effect of devices on learning and productivity when he runs workshops for schools. A response he often gets is, 'Yeah, but when the phone isn't close, students' intelligence goes back to normal, so it's not a problem.' But we don't know what their intelligence could have been if they never had a device. We don't know if it is going back to 'normal'. All we know is it isn't as bad when the device is gone. And when is anyone *not* with a device? Is it okay for our kids to walk around all day, at school, at the park, at friends' places and at home, in second gear? That decrease in intelligence is going to affect their learning and their relationships. It is going to change their decision-making ability and how they empathise with others. It is going to harm their job prospects and their relationships. In short: it matters!

If our intelligence is compromised, how can we expect to hold down a good job or have an intelligent conversation with a friend or loved one? How can we make informed decisions? A reasonable objective measure of intelligence is how well one is performing at university or college. It probably won't surprise you that smartphone use is a good measure of university performance. Professor Lepp and colleagues looked at the GPA scores of a large sample of American college students and their smartphone use. The more students used their phones, the poorer their marks. Not great for job prospects when they graduate (if they graduate).[3]

Have you ever wondered if those map apps on your phone are making you forgetful? It turns out they might be! These apps use GPS to tell us where we are and how to get to our destination. While this is super convenient, it means our brain isn't storing this information anymore. Remember the London taxi drivers? Their brains are great at storing maps because they practise it all the time. But if you rely on your phone, you might forget how you got somewhere.

Imagine this. You're on a family road trip and your kids are in the back seat, asking, 'Are we there yet?' every five minutes. You confidently tell them, 'Just follow the blue line on the map, kids!' But then the GPS signal drops out and you're left staring at a blank screen. Panic sets in as you realise you have no idea where you are. Your kids start giggling and say, 'Mum, Dad, maybe we should have paid more attention to the road signs!'

Some people think it's no big deal because they can always use their phone to get home. But here's the catch: if you don't remember how you got somewhere, you might also forget what you did while you were there. Our memories are like little episodes of our lives, and the place where things happen is a big part of those memories. If we don't remember the place, the memory isn't as strong.

Memories are formed and maintained through practice. How did you learn your maths times tables? You practised many many times. But what exactly are you doing when you practise? You are retrieving the information from your memory. And every time you retrieve it, it's reinforced. The memory gets stronger. If you haven't retrieved a memory for a while, it will get weaker. Pretty obvious, right? Use it or lose it.

But with smartphones, we don't have to retrieve old memories anymore. We can google them! When did you last spend time discussing a fact or past memory with your kids? Do they ever try to remember things, or do they automatically reach for their phone? In the old days, we would sit around trying to remember who sang that song or who scored that goal. These days, we just look it up and we're done with it.

But this means we are not retrieving the memories, so we are not reinforcing or exercising our memory areas.

How many things do you and your kids do on a device rather than in your brain? We don't have to remember, navigate, calculate, socialise or even verbally communicate anymore. It's pretty funny that a device that was invented to enable us to talk over distances is now used to avoid talking! But it's also massively concerning because . . . you know what we're going to say . . . if you don't use it, you lose it!

WHAT IF THE VERY DEVICES DESIGNED TO MAKE US SMARTER ARE MAKING US FORGET HOW TO THINK?

Step into any café, waiting room, school corridor or even your own living room and you'll see a modern ritual unfolding: faces bathed in blue light, fingers scrolling in a rhythm similar to that of violinists in a symphony orchestra. Smartphones hum quietly in pockets and hands, always within reach. We tap them without thinking. We turn to them for directions, definitions, conversions, reminders and reassurance. They're brilliant tools, but the question is: what are they doing to the tool that is our brain?

We now carry more computing power in our pockets than NASA had during the moon landing. Yet at the same time, many of us feel increasingly forgetful, distracted, overwhelmed, even a little foggy. The convenience is undeniable, but so is the cost. We are outsourcing more and more of our mental activity to machines that never sleep. And while this shift may seem subtle, its long-term effect on intelligence, cognition and self-regulation is becoming harder to ignore.

As we've discussed, studies from around the world reveal a troubling trend: for the first time in more than a century, average IQ scores are starting to decline. Alongside this decline, we're seeing a rise in cognitive fatigue, increased forgetfulness and shrinking attention spans. And this isn't just the natural result of stress or ageing. It's the by-product of a world that constantly pulls us away from focused thought, where notifications interrupt our flow, screens splinter our attention, and our minds rarely get the quiet they need to do their best work.

Smartphones were never marketed as devices that would change how we think, but that's *exactly* what they've done. We've become so accustomed to looking things up, checking, calculating and comparing with a tap that we're losing confidence in our ability to hold, recall and process information. And our children, growing up in this environment, are learning to bypass deep thought before it even begins.

Intelligence is not just the ability to access information, it's the ability to synthesise, reflect, question and imagine. These skills require time, quiet and a level of cognitive strain that our devices are designed to avoid. Algorithms favour what's fast, clickable and engaging, not what's complex or ambiguous.

SO WHAT DO WE DO?

We begin by naming the problem, gently and without shame. This isn't about fearmongering or nostalgia for a pre-digital age. It's about awareness. When we notice ourselves reaching for the phone instead of wrestling with a thought, we can pause. When our children forget something and we're tempted to answer for them, we can wait. When a conversation feels disjointed because of constant glances at a screen, we can put it away.

Memory, attention and critical thinking are like muscles: they grow when they're exercised and shrink when they're outsourced. A 2017 study coined the term 'brain drain' to describe the cognitive cost of simply having a smartphone within reach.[4] Even when it's not being used, its presence subtly reduces our working memory and problem-solving ability. In short, just being near our phone makes us think less clearly.

For children, the implications are even greater. Their cognitive systems are still under construction. They need space for deep play, quiet observation, difficult questions and slow problem-solving. These are not optional extras in development, they are essential.

But that doesn't mean removing technology entirely. It means using it on purpose.

We can encourage children to ask before searching. To try to recall instead of immediately googling. To use a notebook instead of a notes app. To feel the joy of solving a problem in their heads and to struggle a little before finding the answer. These small shifts restore confidence in the brain's own power and create the mental friction needed for growth.

Adults need this too. Reading a long article without clicking away. Sitting with a question before checking for a solution. Engaging in conversations that require focus. These practices don't feel urgent, but they are quietly revolutionary in a culture that rewards speed over depth.

As the author James Clear once said, 'Focus is the art of knowing what to ignore.'[5] And when we help children practise that art, we're not just teaching them to concentrate, we're showing them how to value their own thoughts, trust their own minds, and stay present in a world full of noise.

The best part is that even though we've already travelled a long way down the road of technological dependency, it's not too late. Our minds are adaptable, our habits changeable, and our awareness, when we use it, is incredibly powerful.

We're not here to reject technology. We're here to remember that intelligence is far more than just access to information. It's about how we think, what we notice, what we question, and what we remember when the screen goes dark.

THE BENEFITS OF MINDFUL TECH USE FOR MENTAL HEALTH

When we begin to use technology with more intention, we notice something shift. Memory sharpens and attention deepens. It's as if the brain finally has the space it's been craving, like opening a window in a stuffy room. Children start to focus for longer stretches, become more absorbed in their play or learning and feel less jittery. That kind of calm, sustained attention lays the groundwork for deep understanding, not just quick answers.

When children pause before reaching for a device to solve a problem, they give their minds a chance to work things through. Rather than always having an instant solution, they learn to sit with uncertainty, to ask questions and to explore different possibilities. That process might feel slower, even a bit frustrating at times, but it's exactly what builds real thinkers. It strengthens the neural pathways that support critical thinking, resilience and originality; skills that can't be developed by swiping from one video to the next.

There's also a noticeable shift in emotional wellbeing. Constant stimulation, especially from fast-paced or emotionally charged content, can leave children feeling scattered, unsettled or even anxious. But when we make space for quiet, for movement or for unstructured play, it brings balance back into their emotional world. They become more grounded. Sleep improves. And with that, so does their capacity to manage stress, build empathy and engage meaningfully with the people around them.

When the noise quietens down, curiosity has a chance to step forward. Without a steady stream of entertainment filling every gap, children begin to ask more questions, invent more games and follow their ideas wherever they lead. Boredom becomes a doorway, not a problem.

Do you remember those days when we'd build dens under the staircase, dragging cushions and pillows from the sofa, creating entire worlds out of blankets and imagination? Why do those memories feel so vivid, so lasting? Because we lived them. We were moving, creating, laughing and figuring things out, not just watching from the sidelines. These are the kinds of experiences that build strong, healthy, flexible minds. And they're still possible, if we make space for them.

THOUGHT-PROVOKING STATS

The average attention span has dropped from 150 seconds to just forty-seven seconds since the rise of the smartphone.[6]

Having a smartphone nearby, even if silenced and face down, reduces available cognitive capacity.[7]

Students who use smartphones during study sessions score lower on memory and problem-solving tests than those who study without them.[8]

Children who spend more than three hours a day on screens score lower on language and executive functioning tests.[9]

Reading the stats above, we can't help but want to change our ways. Yes, they're stark, but they're included here to remind us that even small, everyday interactions with our devices can reshape how we think and learn. Children, whose brains are still developing, are especially vulnerable and need extra care and attention.

WHAT CAN PARENTS DO?

1. Establish 'daily downtime'

The French philosopher and mathematician Blaise Pascal once said, 'The more we do, the less we remember.'[10] Children thrive when they know there's time carved out each day for quiet focus. Choose a consistent time, perhaps after breakfast or before dinner, when everyone in the house puts their devices away. You might light a candle, put on gentle music and read, journal or work silently together. Over time, this routine builds focus, stillness and self-discipline.

2. Create a bedroom routine that signals rest

Good sleep hygiene starts with the environment. Remove all screens from bedrooms and replace them with books, low lighting and soothing rituals. Run a warm bath, dim the lights or listen to a story on audio together. An old Irish proverb reminds us, 'A good laugh and a long sleep are the best cures in the doctor's book.' Protect this space, physically and emotionally, as a sanctuary for restoration.

3. Designate 'human connection' hours in the weekly calendar

The English poet John Donne wrote, 'No man is an island', and it's never been more true. Choose one evening a week,

perhaps Sunday lunch or a weekday afternoon, for human connection without interruptions. Invite grandparents for tea, cook together without background noise, or even just sit in the garden and chat. Add them to the calendar so they become part of who you are and what you do! The goal isn't to schedule more, but to prioritise human connection.

4. Create a 'Montessori shelf' at home

Set up a simple shelf or corner in your home with calming, hands-on activities that invite focus and creativity for everyone, adults included. Include things like puzzles, tangrams, clay, origami paper, mindful colouring pages or building blocks. Add a notebook or clipboard for sketching, jotting down thoughts or asking questions. Keep the space tidy and rotate materials weekly to keep interest alive. Most importantly, use it yourself. When children see you thinking, making and reflecting, they're far more likely to join in. This isn't just a shelf, it's a gentle daily reminder to slow down and be present.

5. Try something bold together

As the American author Neale Donald Walsch said, 'Life begins at the end of your comfort zone.'[11] The human brain loves novelty. Plan a shared experience that's new for both of you, join a pottery class, go bushwalking with a guidebook, volunteer at a local event or learn a new card game together. The unfamiliar not only stimulates brain growth but also deepens your bond. Most importantly, it teaches your child that being a little unsure is often where the best learning lives.

THE BENEFITS FOR OUR CHILDREN

Although it takes a lot more effort to consciously carve out time for connection in a world designed to distract us, the reality is that when we create healthier boundaries with technology, the benefits for our children – and for ourselves – stretch far beyond the present moment.

The simple and deliberate act of pushing back against the digital tide is one of the most profound investments we can make. As we have seen, the small, consistent choices actively shape the way our children think, feel and grow, giving them the invaluable gift of mental and emotional space to discover who they are without the constant pull of a screen.

By stepping back from the noise, children can rest their minds, strengthen their ability to focus on a single task, and build the foundational qualities of resilience and self-awareness that will carry them into adulthood. The effect of this protected space reaches into every corner of their lives – it influences how they learn in the classroom, how they communicate with empathy and how they ultimately see and value themselves in the world. With the rise of mental health issues associated with screen use evident in every corner of the planet, it's an investment not just in a more peaceful home today, but in the architecture of the people our children are becoming.

Here are five ways everyone will benefit.

Improved memory and retention

Reducing screen time and increasing moments of focus may help children retain what they learn more effectively. When their attention isn't constantly pulled in different directions, they're more likely to store information in their long-term memory and apply it later.

Greater mental agility

Having more time away from devices can improve children's ability to think on their feet, solve problems creatively and approach challenges with flexibility. Without always having an instant answer, they start to rely more on their own reasoning and ideas.

Resilience in the face of challenge

Limiting quick digital escapes may give children more opportunities to sit with uncertainty and frustration, an important part of building resilience. When they work through difficulty instead of avoiding it, they gradually learn that persistence pays off.

Stronger communication skills

Spending more time in face-to-face conversations can support the development of better communication skills. Children may become more tuned into non-verbal cues like tone, facial expression and body language, which helps them understand others and express themselves more clearly.

Healthier long-term relationship with technology

Creating regular boundaries around tech use may help children develop a balanced view of their devices. Over time, they can learn to see screens as helpful tools rather than constant companions, and recognise when it's time to switch off and re-engage with the world around them.

IN SUMMARY

Smartphones and other digital devices are here to stay, but that doesn't mean we have to hand over our intelligence, or our children's, to the glowing lure of convenience. We still get to choose the pace and texture of our lives – the awe, the wonder, the raw beauty of the world that lives outside your front door, not behind a screen. Real learning doesn't come from scrolling; it comes from feeling the wind in your hair, the raindrops sliding down your back, or the gentle surprise of a butterfly landing on your arm.

Life is meant to be lived. As a connected species, we were designed to experience the world through all five senses, not just one. Our opposing thumbs weren't given to us just to scroll through eight-second videos of people dancing in their bedrooms or (admittedly adorable) kittens riding ducks! Those clips have their charm, but they aren't the point of it all.

Our true strength lies in our ability to stop, reflect and think deeply. And if we can gently guide our children back to meaningful, sometimes challenging but always enriching experiences, we give them something far greater than entertainment. We give them the gift of thought. Of curiosity. Of depth. And in doing so, we safeguard not just their future, but the most precious thing of all: the mind itself.

CHAPTER 6

Real connection

When was the last time you managed to chat with a friend without being interrupted by the irresistible siren song of your smartphone? Do you remember when you hung out with someone and didn't sneak a peek at your notifications under the table? Do you ever get the urge to throw your kid's phone at the wall because they won't look up when you ask them to get ready for school? Or maybe you've had a friendship fizzle over a misunderstanding in a text thread (thanks, autocorrect . . .).

Humans are social creatures! We didn't climb to the top of the food chain by running really fast (let's face it, cheetahs win that one), or by being the strongest (move over, elephants), or by having the biggest brain (check out a blue whale). Nope, we got here because we're amazing at making friends, forming groups and, sometimes, yes, organising the world's most complicated carpool schedules. Collaboration, cooperation, empathy, connection: these are the real superpowers that made us the species everyone else in the animal kingdom side-eyes with suspicion.[1]

But socialising isn't as easy as it looks. First, we need to identify who people are and remember all the people we know. No small feat if you've ever tried to recall the name of That Parent From Soccer Practice. Then you're supposed to interpret facial expressions, body language and, if you're really advanced, sarcasm (basically a second language for teenagers). There is complex spoken and written language to deal with. And on top of that, we also rely on voice tone, gestures and the kind of subtle cues that can turn a 'fine' into 'not fine at all'. It's a wonder any of us make it out of a school event with our dignity intact!

In fact, socialising is the most complicated thing we do and we have evolved a big brain to enable us to do it. More of our brain is active when we socialise, face-to-face, than anything else we do. Now think back to the earlier chapters when we explored our brain's ability to adapt and the evidence that we have to 'use it or lose it'. If we want to exercise our brain, if we want to keep it healthy and working maximally, the best thing we can do is sit down and chat with a friend. Honestly, you don't have to study Aristotle – just hang with a mate.

Sitting down and chatting openly and honestly with a close friend or relative on a regular basis has been shown to improve our mental health, increase our life span by more than ten years, decrease the likelihood of getting dementia, and improve our cardiovasculature system and intelligence.[2] But there is an important caveat to this very special exercise: it must be in real life and it must be in the real world.

Perhaps you're wondering why it has to be in real life. Why not online while getting hot and bothered over the latest celeb scandal? Well, in real life, there are heaps of extra cues and stimulation that we don't get when we are online. One of the most important is touch. When we greet someone, we usually touch them in some way (we used to, anyway). In stoic societies we are taught to shake hands, in many European countries they kiss on the cheek, and the Inuit, who have most of their bodies covered from the severe cold, will rub noses. We do this because we have special cells in our skin that detect touch and activate a part of our brain that releases oxytocin. Oxytocin is a very important chemical that makes us feel open, friendly, connected and trusting of those around us. By touching someone when we meet them (appropriately and with consent, of course), we instantly feel more connected.

Another important aspect of meeting face-to-face is that we can see the other person's body language. This is important because we understand how a person is feeling by how they move. If your kid is hunched over and sighing, you know they're not thrilled about folding laundry. If your friend starts mimicking the way you sip your coffee, that's a sign you're in sync. Notice how a group of kids will all end up sitting the same weird way on the couch? That's social mirroring in action. We mimic what others are doing or how they are behaving to show connection. We do this automatically and it is our way of showing that we are part of the same group. It's a vital aspect of socialising.

Add facial expressions, eye contact and voice tone to the mix, and you've got the full social experience. Our brains are built for this; millions of years of evolution have made us experts at picking up the hints and hidden meanings in a well-timed eyebrow raise. And along with these important cues, special chemicals are released in our brain to help us socialise and make us feel connected.

When we're online, we don't have access to many of these important cues. It is harder to know how someone is feeling or what they are thinking. We also don't have the important swarm of chemicals released in our brains to help us socialise in a positive way. Without all of this, we can't easily put the conversation into context or relate to the other person.

Is it any surprise that people are more likely to have misunderstandings and conflicts online? Is it any surprise that people are more likely to be nasty or inappropriate online? Is it any surprise that shaming, bullying, vitriol and abuse are rampant online? People readily agree that many of the things they are willing to say online, they'd never say at school drop-off. As Taylor Swift espouses, if you speak up in public, it's powerful. But if you post it online, it's lame.

It's easy to say stuff online that you wouldn't say to someone's face because you don't have all the important things happening in your brain that have allowed us to connect over millions of years. When you're not face-to-face, your brain's usual social 'brakes' aren't working. Most of these signals disappear. Those helpful brain chemicals? Gone. Suddenly, it's much harder to tell if your friend is joking or if you've somehow started a group text war over pineapple on pizza. No wonder online conversations can go sideways, sometimes spectacularly so.

Why do we keep choosing screens over real-life chats? Simple: it feels easier and safe. No risk of awkward silences, no need to actually wear pants. Being with people, although there are innumerable positives, can be confronting. And all our socialising abilities need to be learned and practised regularly. We need to scare ourselves and take ourselves outside our comfort zone just a bit to learn and progress. Kids (and adults!) need those in-person moments to learn how to read the room, apologise, stand up for themselves and, yes, sometimes survive some heated Monopoly argy-bargy. Sitting in our rooms and communicating via text seems easier but it results in more misunderstandings. Even worse, we miss important opportunities to learn and connect.

There is now a huge amount of research to back up the idea that our use of the smartphone is a real problem. Professor Yalda T. Uhls and colleagues from the University of California Los Angeles (UCLA) showed that simply taking 6th Grade kids on camp for five days without access to devices improved their ability to recognise facial expressions.[3] Just think about that for a minute. These were average kids with 'normal' screen time usage. They didn't do any special cognitive training; they just went on camp! But a camp without devices means time socialising and interaction *in real life*! The fact that this improved their perception of emotions tells us that their starting ability must have been below normal. They didn't need fancy exercises or pricey tutors, just good old-fashioned, device-free socialising.

Even more worrying is that one-year-olds whose caregivers use a smartphone find it harder to recognise facial expressions. Professor Jenny Radesky and colleagues have shown that a caregiver using a smartphone does not respond appropriately to the child. The child falls and the caregiver doesn't look concerned, or the child does something positive and the caregiver doesn't smile.[4] These cues are important during our early years as they help us understand the right response for different actions. This mounting research suggests children are missing out on important social lessons because of our addiction to smartphones.

In the past, we didn't have any choice but to brave potentially challenging social interactions. Now, the smartphone gives us another way to communicate. The issue is that we can't develop the know-how to navigate the complex dance of social communication on a device.

We need to learn subtle signs, body language, facial expressions, prosody and intonation in the voice, pecking orders, and deriving what is 'rad' and what is not (and yes, we know saying 'rad' is not cool anymore!). Although our brains process all these cues automatically, we need to understand what those cues are telling us. If we don't learn what these signals mean, we won't know what to do when they occur.

And remember, social media is not 'social'. It's about watching, not connecting.

So go ahead and use social media to plan your next play date, book club or coffee run. But don't let your thumb do all the connecting – your brain (and your kids) will thank you.

REKINDLING THE FLAME OF REAL CONNECTION IN THE AGE OF SMARTPHONES

When was the last time you had a conversation, fully present, without glancing at your phone, without checking the time, without multitasking? And when was the last time your child saw you do it? If you're being honest, I bet it was a long time ago.

We live in an era of astonishing digital access. We can communicate across continents, share a moment with someone on the other side of the world, or find an answer to almost any question within seconds. And yet, as strange as it sounds, we are becoming *less* connected in the ways that matter most.

In family rooms, at dinner tables, during car rides and on holidays, we often find ourselves physically together but emotionally elsewhere. A study led by Andrew K. Przybylski and Netta Weinstein at the University of Essex found that just the *presence* of a smartphone on the table, even when not in use, is enough to reduce the depth of a conversation.[5] And this subtle disconnection accumulates. When a child feels that their words are competing with a device for our attention, they often stop trying.

Children are incredibly perceptive. They pick up on facial expressions, tone, pauses, posture and eye movement. It's not just *what* we say that matters to them, it's *how* we say it and whether we're truly there when we do. These micro-cues of connection form the foundation of their self-worth and emotional security.

When our children grow up in an environment where full attention is rare, they don't just feel disappointed, they begin to recalibrate what connection even looks like, and that is the saddest part!

This is one of the most understated but serious effects of the digital age. Not only are we distracted, but we are also normalising distraction as part of everyday interaction. The warmth of human presence, the unbroken gaze, the shared silence and the knowing smile are all being diluted by fragmented attention.

Of course, there's no malice in this. We're not trying to ignore our children. In most cases, it's unintentional. We're responding to an email. Checking a work message. Looking up a recipe. But for a child, it feels the same: *I'm not as important as that screen.* And over time, that message leaves a mark.

In a world where screens are always within reach, giving someone your full attention has become rare, but that's exactly what makes it so powerful. These days, being truly present might just be the most genuine act of love we can offer.

Let's not forget, children learn how to connect by watching us. Their ability to make friends, show empathy, resolve conflict and feel a sense of belonging is directly shaped by the quality of their relationships at home. And these relationships are built not through grand gestures, but through small, consistent moments of connection.

When a child tells you about their day and you stop what you're doing, get down to their level and look them in the eye, something powerful happens. You show them that they matter. That their story, however small, is worthy of your full attention. That connection isn't about multitasking, it's about choosing to be fully present with another human being.

We must create opportunities for unstructured, device-free interaction, not just as a rule, but as a rhythm. Family board games, baking together, long walks, time in nature. These activities aren't just wholesome, they're sacred spaces where relationships grow. In those moments, without screens as mediators, we return to the simplicity of what it means to be human: to share time, space and feeling.

Connection isn't always about talking. Sometimes it's about sitting side by side, doing something quietly. Reading together. Gardening. Drawing. These slow, shared silences are just as meaningful as conversation. They say: *I'm here with you, and that's enough.*

In practical terms, we can easily build 'connection rituals' into our day. A shared breakfast without devices. A nightly check-in before bed. A Saturday morning walk, a singalong, or a game of 'spot the red car' on the way to school. These rituals anchor the family in presence. They give children something to count on and something to return to, especially when the world around them feels fast or overwhelming.

None of this means we have to reject technology. We just need to be more intentional about when we put it away. Our children don't need us to be perfect, they just need to know they come first.

Let's also teach them to value real connection by giving them the tools to nurture it themselves. Role-play social situations. Encourage thank-you notes. Teach them to ask questions and listen deeply. Model the kind of friendship you hope they will offer to others.

Because ultimately, no app, platform, or device can teach a child how it feels to be truly seen and known. That is something only we can do. The most profound lessons in life don't arrive as push notifications. They are passed hand to hand, eye to eye, heart to heart.

THE BENEFITS OF ENHANCING SOCIAL CONNECTION

When we choose real connection over convenience, something begins to shift. We start building stronger bonds, not just polite exchanges, but relationships rooted in empathy, trust and deep understanding. Face-to-face interaction allows us to read subtle cues like body language, tone and facial expression, all of which help us tune into what another person is really feeling. And when children experience this kind of connection regularly, they learn how to communicate with kindness, resolve conflicts thoughtfully, and maintain lasting friendships. These are the relationships that help them feel safe, valued and truly seen.

Stepping away from the world of constant comparison that lives on our screens can also ease social anxiety. Online spaces often paint a picture of life that's filtered, curated and far from real. Children (and adults too) can start to feel like they don't measure up. But in the real world, when we sit down for a chat, share a laugh or go for a walk together, we're reminded of our shared humanity. We realise that perfection was never the goal. Just showing up as we are and being accepted for it can do wonders for self-esteem and confidence.

Social connection also plays a huge role in developing emotional intelligence. When we spend time with others in person, whether it's a friend, a family member, or even someone we don't know well, we practise picking up on non-verbal cues: a raised eyebrow, a quiet sigh, a warm smile. These tiny signals help us understand how others are feeling, even when they don't say a word. And as children experience this regularly, they learn to respond with compassion, patience and awareness – skills that shape them into emotionally grounded individuals who can navigate life's ups and downs with empathy.

When we make space for these kinds of interactions in our daily lives, we're not just filling time, we're nurturing something essential. We're helping our children (and ourselves) become more grounded, more self-aware, and more capable of building the kinds of connections that give life meaning. It doesn't require anything fancy, just time, presence and a willingness to be real. And in a world full of digital noise, that quiet, authentic connection is more powerful than ever.

THOUGHT-PROVOKING STATS

Heavy social media use has been linked to mental health issues.

According to a 2024 ACMA-reported study, Australian adolescents spend, on average, around 14.5 hours a week on social media. This use is associated with increased anxiety, depression, social comparison and validation-seeking behaviours.[6]

Eighty-one per cent of NSW school principals reported that student learning improved after mobile phones were

banned in classrooms, and 87 per cent said students were less distracted during lessons.[7]

In 2020, 46 per cent of Australian children aged six to thirteen owned a mobile phone, up from 41 per cent in 2015, indicating growing exposure to technology at younger ages.[8]

Mobile devices can certainly connect us across vast distances, and they allow us to access endless information with a few taps. What they cannot do is replace the messy, joyful process of human interaction. When attention drifts, memories fade and anxiety rises, it serves as a reminder that the richest lessons and the strongest bonds are forged face-to-face, in backyards, classrooms and around kitchen tables.

Those unhurried, device-free moments are not optional extras, they are the fertile ground in which our children's social skills, emotional resilience and love of learning truly take root.

WHAT CAN PARENTS DO?

1. Tech-free days
Choose three evenings a week, say Monday, Wednesday and Friday, for true no-tech time. No phones, tablets, laptops

or even TVs. Place all devices in a basket by the door and reclaim the quiet. These are perfect moments to work on a puzzle together, play a game, share stories from the day, or simply enjoy the comforting hum of home life. As the missionary Jim Elliot reminded us, 'Wherever you are, be all there.'[9] Being fully present is one of the greatest gifts we can offer each other.

2. After-dinner walk and stargaze

Pick one night a week to head out for a 'walk and talk'. Leave your phones behind, step outside and take in the sky, the breeze and each other's company. Even a wander around the block or sitting in the garden opens the door to deeper conversation and a renewed sense of connection. As John Muir once said, 'The clearest way into the Universe is through a forest wilderness.'[10] And sometimes, the clearest way into a child's world is through a quiet walk at dusk.

3. Creative box sessions

Set aside a weekend afternoon to spread out a big box of paper, glue, paints, old magazines, cardboard tubes, and *create* something. It's not about the end result, it's about sharing ideas, solving problems and letting imaginations run wild. As Albert Einstein believed, 'Imagination is more important than knowledge.'[11] These hands-on sessions invite the whole family into a space where everyone gets to explore, invent and connect, no screens required.

4. Family book club

Pick a short, engaging chapter book and take turns reading it aloud, just ten minutes each night. One person starts, another continues. Pause for questions, for laughs, for curious thoughts, or read a book alongside your child, one chapter per week. As the author George R.R. Martin wrote, 'A reader lives a thousand lives before he dies. The man who never reads lives only one.'[12] Reading together like this becomes more than a bedtime routine – it becomes a shared journey full of connection, wonder and story.

5. Screen-free cooking or baking

Once a week, swap screens for spoons. Choose a simple recipe – banana muffins, pasta from scratch, or a fruit platter – and prepare it together. Give each person a role, from chopping to washing up. As Virginia Woolf observed, 'One cannot think well, love well, sleep well, if one has not dined well.'[13] Cooking together nourishes more than just the body; it nourishes connection, cooperation and joy. The best part is you get to eat it all later and enjoy the fruits of your labours!

THE BENEFITS FOR OUR CHILDREN

As we've seen, human beings are wired for connection. It's the thread that holds us together; the very thing our brains and bodies depend on to thrive. From the moment we are born, we look for eyes that meet ours, voices that comfort us and hands that remind us we are not alone. When connection is strong, we flourish. When it is missing, we struggle. For our children, real human connection is more than just important, it's essential.

That's why the small, everyday choices we make at home matter so much. Every shared meal, every story told without a screen nearby, every walk taken side by side is an investment in our children's future. These are the ways they learn to listen, to care, to understand themselves and others. The benefits are some of the most important ones yet.

Deeper emotional resilience

When children spend more time connecting in real life, they get to experience a full range of emotions, disagreements, laughter, awkward moments and apologies, and they learn how to deal with them. It's not always easy, but it's how they build that emotional strength we all want for them: the ability to bounce back, manage big feelings and keep going.

Improved empathy and understanding

You can't learn empathy from a screen. But when children interact face-to-face, they start to notice the small things: how someone's voice changes when they're upset, what a real smile looks like, or when a friend needs support without saying a word. These are the moments that teach children to care, to pause and to understand others more deeply.

Stronger sense of belonging

When a child feels listened to – *really* listened to – they start to believe that they matter. Not because of how many likes they got or how clever their post was, but because someone looked them in the eye and showed up for them. That's what builds a true sense of belonging and security.

Greater confidence in communication

The more children practise talking and listening in real life, the more confident they become. Whether they're explaining an idea, telling a story or working through a disagreement, these everyday chats help them find their voice and learn how to listen. It's not about being perfect, it's about showing up and having a go.

Balanced relationship with technology

When children see the value of real connection, they begin to understand that screens can be helpful, but they're not the whole world. They start to realise that some of the best things in life don't come with notifications. They learn to reach for people first and devices second.

IN SUMMARY

The glow of a screen might be tempting; it's easy, it's convenient, it's always there. But the real magic? You find that in the warmth of face-to-face connection. A look across the table. A shared laugh. A quiet moment that says, 'I see you.' That's what builds relationships and shapes lives.

As the grown-ups in the room, we have a powerful role to play. Not in being perfect, but in being present. When we set boundaries around screen time, talk openly about connection and make time for real-world moments, walks, chats, games and shared silences, we show our children that they matter more than any message on a screen.

So let's fill our homes with the sound of *real* laughter. Let empathy grow through honest conversations.

Let confidence and trust take root in those everyday interactions that might seem small, but actually mean everything.

Because in the end, it won't be the selfies or the screen time they remember, it'll be the way we made them feel. The stories we told. The time we gave. The way we looked up, not down, when they needed us most. And that's the legacy worth leaving, one smile, one story, one real connection at a time.

CHAPTER 7

Feeling sad

As parents, we always want what's best for our kids and that means paying attention to their friendships, their feelings and, increasingly, how technology influences their lives. Just like we'd encourage them to distance themselves from people who consistently make them feel bad, it's just as important to think about how devices and social media make them feel.

Do your kids sometimes feel sad? Do they occasionally feel lonely? Do they worry from time to time? Or you may be thinking that they have these feelings *all the time*? Experiencing negative feelings occasionally is a normal part of life. It's our brain's way of warning us that there is potentially something, someone, or a behaviour that we are doing that could be affecting us in a negative way. Perhaps there's something we need to change. But having these feelings all the time means that there is something that we're not dealing with.

We need to listen to our brain! If a friend makes us feel sad whenever we're around them, we might question what sort of friend they are. If someone is not nice to us and we feel miserable in their company, would we want to hang out with them? If just thinking about spending time with someone makes us anxious or worried, wouldn't we want to minimise that time? Our brains create negative emotions as a mechanism to tell us that a situation or a person probably isn't good for us. Maybe we should spend less time with them and more time with friends who make us feel happy. People we like being around.

Have you ever noticed how you feel after spending time on your phone, or have you checked in with your child about what they're experiencing online? Sometimes after scrolling social media or watching online videos, we feel anxious or down. It's important to listen to those feelings. Our brains are trying to tell us something.

Did you know that loneliness, anxiety, depression, stress and suicide are at an all-time high? This increase in negative emotions is directly correlated with the increase in device use.

Professor Jean Twenge and her colleagues showed that since 2010 there has been a dramatic increase in mental health issues among teenagers.[1] They have studied millions of people across the world from all age groups and shown that the significant increase in mental health problems across all age groups is associated with device use. Quite simply, the more time we spend on our devices, the more likely we are to feel stressed and unhappy.

You may have heard new words popping up like 'unfriending', 'ghosting', 'catfishing' and 'cyberbullying', which all describe negative behaviours that have become more common with the use of devices. Unfortunately, it's much easier for people to be mean or inappropriate when they're behind a screen, not seeing the real-world effects their words or actions have on others. These experiences are very hurtful and are contributing to the rise in mental health problems.

Worry is often the first step on the path to mental health issues. In psychology we colloquially talk about the 'worried well'. In cyberspace there's a new term for a special type of worry, FOMO (Fear Of Missing Out). This isn't about missing a family event or a friend's birthday, it's about feeling you have to check every new meme, video or post just to keep up. It's about worrying that you won't be the first to forward a funny meme, like a cool video, comment on a rad post, or whatever. Not only do our kids have to worry about getting to school on time, getting their homework done, having time for their friends, wearing the right clothes and all the real things that happen in real life, they now have the added stress of keeping up with what's happening online.

Or do they? Is it really *that* important?

Social media companies use clever techniques to keep us coming back for more, and this can make feelings of loneliness worse. A recent study of hundreds of thousands of teens showed that loneliness has been increasing at an alarming rate.[2] Teens today feel lonely at school and lonely at home. And that increase in loneliness goes hand in hand with access and use of devices. The more time someone spends on their device, the lonelier they feel. And the more friends they have on social media, the fewer friends they have in real life. Are virtual friends going to help them when something goes wrong? Sit with them when they're upset? Convince them to go out and have fun when things are tough?

This is why real-world, in-person friendships are so important. Spending time face-to-face with friends helps children (and adults!) lower stress and boosts overall mental health. Being glued to a screen, on the other hand, raises stress levels, no matter what you're doing. Hanging out with a friend in real life is better for our mental wellbeing than any device or drug!

You would have to have been living on Mars not to have heard about the increase in anxiety and depression in society over the past few years. While it is a major issue for all age groups, it is seen most dramatically in young adults and teens. And yes, there is a huge amount of research now showing a link between anxiety and depression and device use. There was a study conducted in China where the researchers had access to participants who didn't have social media accounts. When they signed these participants up to social media accounts, they showed significant increases in anxiety and depression after only a few weeks.[3] Crazy, right? A few weeks on social media and your mental health takes a dive!

Have you or your kids ever been bullied on social media? Have they had to deal with trolls or cyberbullies? It can be devastating. In Spain they banned smartphones from schools in some provinces but not others, which resulted in an interesting natural experiment that was studied by Professor Pilar Beneito López and his colleagues. In areas where phones were banned, there was a significant decrease in both cyberbullying (not surprising) as well as 'old-school' bullying. Restricting phones also had a positive effect on mental health and academic outcomes.[4]

Let's go back to that friend who makes you feel sad whenever you hang out with them. Is this a person you should be spending lots of time with? Probably not. And we know that after spending time on devices, people feel more depressed than they did before they started scrolling. The 'TikTok brain' is a term used to describe the negative effects of social media on teens. So why do we do it to ourselves? Maybe it's time to rethink our relationship with social media and how we use our devices.

So what does this all mean for our families? It's worth taking a closer look at how much time our children, and we, as parents, spend on screens, and how it makes us feel. If our children seem unhappy after scrolling or checking messages, it might be a sign to make some changes.

Ultimately, just as we want our kids to spend time with friends who lift them up, we should help them develop a healthy relationship with technology. Encouraging real-life connections, setting boundaries around device use and having open conversations about what they're experiencing online can make all the difference.

Let's work together to support our children in making choices that lead to happier, healthier lives, both online and off.

BEYOND THE BLUE LIGHT — TURNING OFF THE POWER TO REKINDLE JOY

We're living in the most connected era in human history, so why are so many children feeling more isolated, more anxious and less joyful than ever before?

Each morning, millions of kids begin their day not with a hug or a chat at the breakfast table, but with the soft glow of a screen. Teenagers now spend more than 8.5 hours a day on their digital devices, not including time spent on schoolwork. For children aged eight to twelve, it's around 5.5 hours.[5] We often speak of digital connection, but what we are seeing more and more is digital *substitution*; screens replacing moments of play, of silence and of shared wonder.

It's not just about screen time. It's about what's being *crowded out*.

Joy used to come from building things with our hands, getting muddy in the garden and laughing until our bellies ached with friends we could reach out and touch. Now, joy is often filtered, delayed and approved by an algorithm. Children scroll through endless reels of other people's lives, chasing moments that aren't real, comparing themselves to images that have been edited, curated and cropped to perfection. And they feel, often without knowing why, that they're not enough.

Studies have drawn a clear line between these digital habits and mental health. Professor Jean Twenge discovered a significant correlation between increased screen time, especially time spent on social media, and rising levels of depression and loneliness in children and teens. Between 2010 and 2019, rates of depressive symptoms among US adolescents rose by over 60 per cent, with the steepest rise seen among those who spent the most time online.[6]

And while technology itself isn't inherently bad, the *way* it is used often interferes with the conditions that nurture emotional wellbeing: genuine relationships, spontaneous play, physical movement and time in nature.

In fact, the World Health Organization has now formally recognised *gaming disorder* and *problematic screen use* as emerging concerns in childhood development.[7] Meanwhile, the Royal College of Paediatrics and Child Health notes that higher screen time usage is associated with poorer sleep, reduced self-esteem and lower levels of happiness, especially when digital use replaces real-life connection.[8]

So what does joy look like now? And more importantly, how do we help our children find it again? It doesn't live in beeps and clicks, endless scrolling, or performance for an invisible audience. Joy is relational. It's sensory. It's human. It's the giggle that bursts out during a silly moment. The dirt under the fingernails after an afternoon spent digging in the garden. The satisfaction of finishing a drawing, a puzzle or a book. Joy is the glow on a child's face when they realise someone is truly listening to them. These are not small things. They are the building blocks of emotional health.

Real joy, unlike digital entertainment, isn't manufactured. It's discovered. And it often shows up when children have space to be themselves, unwatched, unscored and unfiltered. As adults, we are the gatekeepers of this space.

We can't shield our kids from the digital world, but we *can* help them navigate their way through it. We can model what it looks like to choose presence over performance. To put our phones down. To find joy in the real world. If our mission is for children to engage meaningfully with the world around them, then we must model that engagement too. Simple invitations like, 'Shall we go outside together?' or 'Do you want to bake something together?' or 'Wanna make a card for Grandma?' aren't just ways to pass the time, they're quiet, radical acts in a world that's constantly trying to pull our kids away from what matters.

We can also give them tools to build real-world joy themselves. Teach them how to make a friend. How to write a story, take care of a pet, start a project or help a neighbour. These activities build confidence, purpose and connection; things no algorithm can offer, but important moments that they will remember for a lifetime.

Children who feel seen, trusted and loved don't need to chase validation online. They already know they belong.

There's a quote by Fred Rogers that feels more relevant today than ever. 'Play is often talked about as if it were a relief from serious learning. But for children, play is serious learning. Play is really the work of childhood.'[9]

You see, joy isn't a luxury and it never has been; it's a *necessity*. It protects mental health. It fosters resilience. It helps children bounce back from setbacks and stay hopeful in hard times. And when joy is rooted in real life, it becomes something children carry with them, not something they chase on a screen.

We can't turn back the clock. But we can create homes, classrooms and communities where children don't feel the need to escape. Places where they're free to be curious, messy, creative and loved exactly as they are.

Because if we want our children to thrive in this world, not just survive it, they need more than stimulation. They need joy. The real kind.

THE BENEFITS OF A DIGITAL DETOX

When we take a break from the constant stream of pings, alerts and scrolling, something subtle but powerful begins to happen: our nervous system starts to calm. That underlying tension we didn't even realise was there begins to ease. Stress levels drop, focus returns, and the pace of life slows just enough for us to catch our breath. It's not about rejecting technology altogether, but about creating space for stillness. When we disconnect, even briefly, we give our minds a chance to reset and our children a chance to experience what it feels like to be fully present.

Taking time away from screens also opens the door to richer, more meaningful relationships. Without digital distractions, conversations grow deeper, eye contact lingers a little longer, and there's room for shared laughter, thoughtfulness and spontaneous connection. It's in these quiet, everyday moments – helping with dinner, walking the dog, telling stories at bedtime – that real connection flourishes. And as children experience this more often, they begin to understand that their value isn't tied to likes or views or followers, but to how they make others feel and how deeply they are loved.

Perhaps most importantly, stepping away from the curated world of social media helps kids develop a more grounded sense of self. Without the pressure to perform or compare, they have the freedom to explore who they are without judgement. They begin to measure their worth by their own inner compass, rather than someone else's highlight reel. In that space, confidence grows; not the kind that comes from attention or approval, but the quiet, steady kind that comes from knowing you are enough, just as you are.

The benefits go beyond emotional wellbeing; school performance often improves too. Children who sleep better, focus longer and feel less anxious learn more effectively. When their minds aren't preoccupied with online drama or dopamine-fuelled distractions, they can concentrate in class, retain what they've learned and engage more deeply with their studies. Reduced screen time has been linked with better memory, stronger problem-solving skills and higher academic outcomes. More importantly, it supports positive mental health, and results in less anxiety, fewer mood swings and a stronger sense of emotional balance. Because when children feel good, they do better. Not just in school, but in life.

THOUGHT-PROVOKING STATS

Forty-six per cent of Canadians aged sixteen to twenty-four who spend seven or more hours per day on personal screen time report experiencing symptoms of moderate to severe anxiety.[10]

Adolescents aged twelve to seventeen who spend twenty-one or more hours a week on their devices report significantly lower levels of life satisfaction, autonomy and happiness.[11]

Teenagers who spend more than three hours per day on their devices are 60 per cent more likely to report feeling persistently sad or hopeless.[12]

These numbers should spark more than concern, they should spark action. If nearly half of our young people who spend extended time on their devices are experiencing anxiety, and if prolonged device use is leaving so many of them feeling flat, disconnected and emotionally adrift, then we need to pause and ask: what are we doing to prepare our children for this world they've inherited?

As families, we can't just tell children to 'get off their phones'. We need to teach them *why* it matters. We need to help them understand how technology affects not just their eyes and posture, but their minds, their sleep, their relationships and their sense of self. This is about educating the *whole child*; body, mind and heart. We wouldn't let our children walk into a dangerous situation without support or awareness, and yet we send them into the online world without the scaffolding to truly protect themselves.

It starts with open conversations. With modelling boundaries around our own screen use. With helping children notice how they *feel* after scrolling, and what it's like to be present in the real world instead. We can build daily habits that foster balance and connection, screen-free meals, outdoor adventures, creative downtime, or just space for boredom and daydreaming. These are not old-fashioned ideas. They're acts of protection. They're investments in our children's long-term wellbeing. Because if we want our children to thrive, not just survive, in a digital world, we must do more than limit their screen time. We must nurture the wisdom, habits and the inner compass they will carry long after we're no longer there to guide them.

WHAT CAN PARENTS DO?

1. Sacred screen-free mealtimes

'Food is our common ground, a universal experience,' said chef and author James Beard, and he was right.[13] Meals offer a rare chance in the day to gather, connect and simply *be* with one another. Make every breakfast, lunch or dinner a screen-free zone. Leave the phones in another room and let the table become a place for stories, laughter and the simple comfort of shared presence. It's not about perfection, it's about togetherness.

2. Evening tech curfew

There's something powerful about setting a consistent, gentle boundary, like a family tech cut-off at 8 p.m. 'Sleep is the golden chain that ties health and our bodies together,' wrote Charles Dickens, and it starts long before heads hit pillows.[14] Replace late-night scrolling with winding-down rituals: reading a book, chatting about the day, or planning tomorrow. This small shift can bring peace to the whole household.

3. Screen-time reflection

What if children tracked their own screen use, not as a punishment, but as a path to understanding? Set up a simple weekly challenge where each family member logs their daily screen time and pairs it with a short mood diary. At the end of the week, gather to reflect: when did you feel most energised? When did you feel low? What patterns do you notice? As Confucius wisely said, 'What I hear, I forget; what I see, I remember; what I do, I understand.'[15] This act of noticing time, feelings and choices can open the door to powerful conversations and healthier habits.

4. Weekly walk and talk

There's no pressure on a walk, no script, no expectations, just space. A simple stroll after school or dinner gives children room to think, breathe and speak when they're ready. 'An early-morning walk is a blessing for the whole day,' said Henry David Thoreau, but even at dusk, the same truth applies.[16] These small, screen-free rituals remind children that they are worth your time, your attention and your footsteps!

5. Family screen time!

As author Brené Brown reminds us, 'Connection is why we're here; it's what gives purpose and meaning to our lives.'[17] So instead of everyone retreating into their individual screens,

try one shared digital window each week, watch a film together, listen to a podcast, or follow a creative tutorial as a team. It's not about banning technology, but using it intentionally, together, not apart.

THE BENEFITS FOR OUR CHILDREN

One of the biggest challenges we face today is the quiet toll that too much screen time takes on our children's mental health and wellbeing. We see the signs all around us: more anxiety, more loneliness, more restless sleep, and children struggling to manage big feelings. None of this is because our children are weak. It is because their growing brains and hearts were never designed to spend so much time staring at a device.

When screens replace face-to-face connection, play, rest and the chance to simply be, children miss out on the very experiences that make them feel alive, safe and connected. The good news is that we are *not* powerless. By making small, intentional changes and gently guiding our families towards healthier habits, we can give back what screens have taken away. Here are some of the benefits your kids will experience in their emotional wellbeing, along with other powerful effects that come when we place connection and presence at the centre of family life.

Reduced feelings of loneliness and anxiety

When children spend more time in genuine connection, through play, conversation or shared experiences, they build a sense of belonging that screens alone can't offer. Human interaction provides emotional safety, helping them feel seen, heard and valued. This kind of emotional grounding acts as a buffer against the rising tide of anxiety and loneliness that so many young people face today.

A stronger sense of self

Offline time gives children the space to discover who they are, without the pressure to perform, compare or edit themselves for an audience. Real experiences, real friendships and real-world challenges help form authentic confidence and self-worth. Over time, children learn to value themselves not for how many likes they receive, but for their ideas, actions and character.

Improved mental health and emotional regulation

Reducing passive screen time has been consistently linked to lower rates of depression, anxiety and poor sleep. Children who step back from overstimulation have more time for physical activity, rest, imagination and reflection – all vital ingredients for emotional stability. With fewer digital distractions, they're better able to focus, cope with stress and bounce back from setbacks.

Greater capacity for empathy and compassion

Screens can't replace the subtle learning that comes from real human interaction, the kind where children notice a friend's tone, a sibling's expression, or the shift in someone's mood. These small, everyday moments teach them to read emotional cues, to listen fully and to care deeply. Over time, this builds the foundation for meaningful, lasting relationships based on empathy and understanding.

Greater emotional awareness and self-regulation

When children step away from constant stimulation, they begin to notice how they feel, not just in the moment, but over time. They start to recognise the connection between what they do and how it affects their mood, energy and focus. With gentle guidance, they can learn to ask themselves: do I feel calm or restless? Energised or drained? Connected or alone? These simple reflections empower them to take action, whether it's stepping outside for fresh air, reaching out to a friend, or simply taking a break. Over time, they develop an inner compass for wellbeing, learning to manage their emotions with intention and maturity.

IN SUMMARY

The glow of a screen may pull at our children's attention, but the deeper light, the one that truly sustains them, is found elsewhere. It's in the small things: the way someone listens without distraction, the feel of sun on skin, the laughter that comes from nowhere and needs no audience. These are the moments that anchor a life.

If we want our children to live with depth, not just distraction, then we must help them return to themselves. To know their own minds. To trust how they feel. To understand that their worth isn't measured in views, likes or followers, but in how they show up in the world, with kindness, curiosity and courage.

This is not about banning devices. It's about lifting our children's gaze, so they can see what's real, what matters and what lasts. It's about teaching them that joy doesn't come from being watched, but from being fully awake to the world around them.

So, as parents and caregivers, we go first. We put our phones down. We invite conversation. We model what it means to be present. And in doing so, we give our kids permission to do the same, to step into life with open eyes, open hearts and the quiet confidence that they don't need to chase the light. It's already in them.

CHAPTER 8

21st-century skills

When you were a kid, did you know what you wanted to be when you grew up? And if you did, did it stick, or did it change every few months? Did you ever think about what important skills would be needed to perform well in that role? Or what you would need to learn to become an expert in that area?

If you're like most parents, you've probably witnessed your child cycle through a dizzying list of dream jobs before the age of ten. One day they're saving the planet as a scientist; the next, they're running a bakery for dogs. But here's the kicker: no matter what career path they imagine or what fascinating combo they invent, there's a common thread; the skills they'll need to actually survive in the grown-up world.

We've all heard the chatter about '21st-century skills'. Turn on breakfast TV and inevitably a 'futurist' will appear having looked into their crystal ball. If you've attended a school assembly, glanced at an education blog, or even just stood near a group of teachers at a coffee shop, you've probably heard the list: Communication! Collaboration! Leadership! Emotional intelligence! Empathy! Creativity! Critical thinking!

But you know what most people forget? The almighty, under-appreciated, absolutely essential skill of *brain health*. That's right. Keeping your child's brain in working order is the secret sauce. Because, spoiler alert, you can't be a genius inventor or a dazzling public speaker if your brain is running on empty.

Think about it: even if your child grows up to be a super-star athlete, it's their brain pulling the strings, quite literally. The brain keeps all those muscle routines humming, keeps stress from sending them running off the field, and helps them make smart choices when it's crunch time. And let's not forget the endless parade of decisions, split-second moves and 'what just happened?' moments that come with every major event.

And what if your child's future is less 'Olympic gold' and more 'friendly carpenter'? Brain health is still the star of the show. A good carpenter doesn't just hammer in nails. They juggle customers, crunch the numbers, read blueprints, improvise when things (inevitably) go sideways, maybe even run a business, wrangle taxes and occasionally have to explain to a client why a tree house doesn't need a jacuzzi. All of that takes a brain firing on all cylinders, not one that's been fried by a weekend of *Minecraft* marathons.

The point is: whatever your kids want to do, a healthy brain is not just going to help them get there, it is *essential*. And, as a bonus, all those other 21st-century skills like empathy, leadership, creativity and so on rely on brains that are functional. So protecting and nurturing the old grey matter really does matter.

But what about the ever-present 'ICT skills', otherwise known as getting really good at using devices? Raise your hand if you've been told your kid needs more screen time 'because it's important for the future'. Here's the plot twist: modern tech is so user-friendly, it doesn't take thirteen years at school to master. Give a six-year-old a smartphone, a tablet or a laptop and watch them figure out more than you can in a few hours. No PhD required.

The reason devices are so ubiquitous in society these days is that they are super easy to use. Anyone can pick up a smartphone and get the hang of it in a matter of minutes. These ICT skills can be acquired very quickly.

And what about programming? I'm sure you've seen the coding camps, but a lot of those jobs are actually being outsourced, and now, with AI like ChatGPT, you can ask a computer to write code for you. (I wish I'd had that in my programming days!) The bottom line is learning to use tech is more like learning to ride a bike; useful, but not a lifelong quest.

What about working for a big tech company? Surely that's the dream for a lot of young people. Well, according to Laszlo Bock, former Head of People at Google, they're not looking for people who can swipe the fastest or code in the most languages. They hire people who are bright, curious and can learn, because they're more likely to come up with a new solution that the world hasn't seen before. Google look for attributes like 'enjoying fun, a certain dose of intellectual humility, a strong measure of conscientiousness, comfort with ambiguity, and evidence that you've taken some courageous or interesting paths'.[1] Hang on, not a single one of those can be learned or experienced on a device! That's right, Google values people who have gone out into the real world and experienced life and what it has to offer.

So if you're anxious about preparing your kids for the future, relax. The magic formula isn't 'more device time', despite what big tech would have us believe. It's real-world experiences, brain-healthy activities and honest-to-goodness human interaction. You know, talking to people face-to-face, doing chores, getting bored and figuring out how to un-bore themselves.

Help your kids manage their screen time, encourage them to try new things, let them learn from mistakes and remind them (fondly, with just a hint of irony) that the best skills are learned in the wild, not in front of a glowing rectangle. The future will thank you and so will their brains.

WHY BRAIN HEALTH IS THE 21ST-CENTURY SKILL THAT MATTERS MOST

If a child can't think clearly, focus deeply or regulate their emotions, does it really matter how well they can code, pitch a product or solve an equation?

We often avoid this question because it disrupts the metrics we've come to rely on. But in moments of real struggle – the anxiety before school, the meltdowns in class, the quiet disengagement at the dinner table – it becomes impossible to ignore. These are not isolated incidents. They are symptoms of something deeper: a growing disconnect between the demands we place on children and the biological reality of what their brains can sustain.

There is no shortage of conversation around 'future-ready' education. From robotics labs and entrepreneurial pitch days to coding camps and digital portfolios, schools are full of initiatives designed to build 21st-century skills. And yet, within all this preparation, we are often missing the one thing that underpins everything else: a healthy, well-functioning brain.

We rarely stop to ask: what good is critical thinking, creativity or collaboration if the brain behind those skills is overwhelmed, exhausted or dysregulated? What happens when we prioritise performance without securing the cognitive foundation it depends on?

The truth is, we are raising children in an environment that is cognitively and emotionally overstimulating. Their brains are being asked to adapt to conditions they were never designed for; constant notifications, fragmented attention, limited movement and increasing pressure to produce and perform. All while being bombarded by the curated lives of others through screens that rarely switch off.

And still, we push forward as though the brain will adjust. But it won't.

Neuroscience tells us that the habits and environments children experience today are literally shaping the structure and function of their brains. Sleep patterns, physical activity, screen time and social connection are not minor lifestyle factors. They are key determinants of how the brain grows and operates across a lifetime.

The Adolescent Brain Cognitive Development Study has shown that children who spend more than seven hours a day on screens exhibit reduced grey matter in areas responsible for language and executive functioning.[2] At the same time, over 70 per cent of teenagers are not getting enough sleep, a factor known to impair memory, emotional regulation and learning.[3] These statistics should not merely alarm us, they should compel us to act.

So we must ask ourselves: are we educating for the future or exhausting our children before they even get there?

Because a child with a dysregulated nervous system, a chronically tired mind, or a habit of digital distraction may still show up in class, but they're not learning deeply. They're not connecting meaningfully. And they're not thriving. If we truly care about preparing children for life, not just tests or jobs, we need to reorient the conversation. Not around better tech, but around better conditions. Not more pressure, but more protection.

Brain health isn't optional. It's our foundation. And if we want our children to be capable of thinking critically, solving complex problems, leading with empathy, or adapting to change – or just being able to handle the ebbs and flows of life – then we need to create environments that allow their brains to function at their best.

We begin with some honest questions:

- Do our school schedules respect the need for rest, movement and outdoor time?

- Are we treating sleep as a health priority or as an inconvenience?
- Do we allow room for boredom, creativity and silence, or are we filling every space with stimulation?
- Are we teaching children how their brains work and how they can care for them?

The brain is not a passive container to be filled; it's an active organ that requires rhythm, regulation and respect.

Psychiatrist Dr Bruce Perry reminds us, 'The most powerful tool we have to shape the brain is the relationship.'[4] When children feel safe, connected and supported by steady, caring adults, their brain is more receptive to learning, growth and change. And yet, how often do we prioritise real connection in our classrooms and homes?

We also need to stop treating brain health and mental health as separate conversations. Rising anxiety, attention difficulties and emotional distress in young people are not isolated disorders, they are responses to environments that push too hard and replenish too little. If a child is struggling, we must stop blaming them and start examining the system.

A 2023 study by the Centre for Addiction and Mental Health (CAMH) found that one in three children in high screen-use households displayed signs of moderate to severe depression. However, those who maintained consistent sleep, physical activity and strong in-person relationships reported significantly better mental and cognitive outcomes, even when their academic achievement was considered average.[5]

So again, we must ask: what do we value more, short-term academic performance or long-term wellbeing and adaptability? Because a child who can regulate their emotions, think clearly, manage stress and maintain healthy relationships is going to be far better prepared for an uncertain world than a child who has simply mastered a skill list.

So what actually supports brain health?

- Consistent, quality sleep; the foundation of cognitive restoration and emotional balance.
- Daily physical movement, which fuels focus, relieves stress and strengthens neural connections.
- Boundaries around screens and stimulation to protect against overload and preserve attention.
- Strong, trusting relationships with adults who model emotional regulation and presence.
- Unstructured time for creativity, play and rest, to process, imagine and reset.
- Purposeful, age-appropriate challenges; not pressure, but meaningful engagement.

These aren't 'extras'. They are essential conditions for a developing brain. Without them, no amount of academic intervention will produce the results we say we want. In the end, the brain can only give what it has been given the time and space to build.

So how do we define success?

Not by how quickly a child can learn, but by how deeply they can engage. By how well they can manage themselves under stress. By how thoughtfully they respond to others. By how clearly they think, even when life gets messy. These are the markers of future-ready children.

For many kids, and for many adults too, the constant stream of reels, shorts and sound bites on social media sends a clear message: success means relentless growth, constant productivity and working around the clock. The world seems to reward the hustle. But at what cost?

Progress should *never* come at the expense of a healthy mind.

A child should grow up knowing that their brain is not a machine to be pushed harder, faster, longer; but a living, responsive part of who they are. It needs rhythm. It needs rest. It needs care. True strength lies not just in knowing how to focus, but in knowing when to pause. Not just in reaching out, but when to turn inward. These are the skills that help a child remain grounded in a world that rarely stops moving.

Resilience isn't built through exhaustion. It's built through balance.

Perhaps it's time we stop asking only, 'What do we want our children to achieve?' and begin asking, 'What kind of minds will they need in order to live well?'

Because the most vital skill they'll carry into the 21st century won't come from a device, an app or even a textbook. It will be their ability to recognise the value of their own mind and to protect it. And when we guide them to care for that mind, not through fear or control, but through understanding, we're not just preparing them for what lies ahead. We're trusting them to build something better.

THE BENEFITS OF PRIORITISING BRAIN HEALTH AND MENTAL WELLNESS

When we prioritise brain health in our homes, classrooms and communities, we do more than protect children from harm; we give everyone the tools to live with more clarity, balance and purpose.

Reducing our dependence on devices helps protect the brain from the effects of digital overstimulation. So many of the apps we use daily are designed to hold our attention, not serve our wellbeing. By becoming more aware of how these platforms are engineered and by setting intentional boundaries, we reduce the risk of digital dependency and preserve our ability to focus, reflect and truly rest.

Just as importantly, we create a buffer against rising mental health challenges. The evidence is clear: excessive screen time is linked to increased rates of anxiety, depression and attention difficulties. When we build healthier relationships with technology, we're not simply avoiding risk, we're actively strengthening our emotional resilience. We make space for stillness, for human connection and for the quiet processing the brain so deeply needs.

And when we feed the brain what it actually thrives on – time in nature, hands-on creative work, real conversations, mindfulness and movement – we see the difference. Not just in children, but in ourselves. We become more present. More emotionally attuned. More able to weather life's demands with grace and clarity. These practices don't just support short-term calm, they lay the groundwork for lifelong cognitive strength and emotional wellbeing.

Prioritising brain health isn't just a protective measure. It's an invitation to live more consciously. To design our days around what nourishes us, not just what distracts us.

THOUGHT-PROVOKING STATS

Only 20 per cent of UK children aged eleven to seventeen meet the recommended one hour of daily physical activity, according to NHS Digital, affecting both brain development and mental wellbeing.[6]

American teenagers who spend more than seven hours a day on screens are twice as likely to be diagnosed with anxiety and depression compared to those who use screens moderately.[7]

Children who spend more than two hours a day on screens score lower on language and thinking tests than children who engage in more offline activities.[8]

Many of us can still remember what it felt like to spend full days outdoors, racing our bikes through the neighbourhood, climbing trees, building cubbies, lying in the grass with friends from sunrise to sunset. Back then, the day didn't revolve around a screen. It revolved around movement, imagination and connection. We explored, we created, we got bored, and that boredom gave birth to adventure.

But today, something has shifted.

Children are spending less and less time outside. In fact, many barely set foot outdoors during the week. Not because they've lost the desire to play, but because parents have become overprotective and technology has taken hold. Screen-based entertainment has filled every spare moment.

What once belonged to dirt, laughter and daydreams now belongs to algorithms, curated content and endless scrolls.

This isn't just a change in habits, it's a warning sign.

As stated above, only 20 per cent of UK children aged eleven to seventeen meet the recommended daily hour of physical activity.[9] That means four out of five British kids are missing a key ingredient for healthy brain development and emotional regulation. In the US, teens who spend more than seven hours a day on screens are *twice as likely* to be diagnosed with anxiety or depression. And children exposed to more than two hours of screen time per day are showing *lower performance* on language and thinking tests, compared to their peers who engage more in offline activities.[10]

These aren't just statistics, they are an urgent call for reflection.

Are we building environments that nurture strong, healthy, resilient minds? Or are we feeding a culture that keeps children overstimulated and undernourished, mentally, physically and emotionally?

Ensuring that children have time to move their bodies, to play freely, to be bored, to rest and to connect face-to-face is no longer optional. It is essential. This is not about rejecting technology altogether, it's about reclaiming balance. Because when the brain is constantly bombarded but rarely given time to reset, everything else begins to break down; focus, memory, mood, creativity and joy.

If we truly want our kids to thrive, we need to stop treating these moments of movement, rest and real-world play as 'extras'. They are not. They are the foundations. They are the brain's natural operating conditions. Without them, no app, no academic success, no test score can compensate.

This moment calls for honesty and courage. Are we willing to turn off the devices, step outside and give children the space to grow in the ways nature intended? Are we ready to prioritise brain health not just in theory, but in practice? If we don't, we risk raising a generation that is digitally fluent but emotionally fatigued, connected to everything except themselves.

And if we do? We give children back what the screens have taken: their sense of wonder, their capacity for deep thought, their ability to feel fully alive in the world around them.

WHAT CAN PARENTS DO?

1.   Establish a consistent sleep–wake rhythm

Keep bedtimes and wake times steady, even on weekends. This stabilises your child's circadian rhythm, helping the brain consolidate memory, regulate emotions and support focus throughout the day. Start each morning by opening the curtains and absorbing a few minutes of sunlight. This simple ritual triggers the body's internal clock. Neuroscientist Matthew Walker, author of *Why We Sleep*, notes that 'the shorter your sleep, the shorter your lifespan'.[11] Helping your family sleep well isn't a routine choice, it's a long-term investment in mental and physical health.

2. Mindfulness Mondays

Begin the week with a shared five-minute moment of stillness. Sit quietly with your child, breathing slowly and paying attention to the breath or gentle sounds in the room. This small act activates the prefrontal cortex, which supports attention, empathy and emotional control. Jon Kabat-Zinn, pioneer of modern mindfulness-based stress reduction, reminds us, 'Mindfulness means paying attention in a particular way: on purpose, in the present moment, and non-judgmentally.'[12] Teaching children to pause is a gift they'll carry into every stressful moment life throws at them.

3. Morning affirmations

Just before leaving for school, exchange a genuine, positive affirmation, something heartfelt like, 'You're brave when you try new things' or 'I love how you notice the little details'.

Spoken aloud, affirmations activate the brain's reward circuitry and strengthen emotional resilience. In *The Science of Positivity*, Loretta Graziano Breuning writes, 'Positive feedback builds neural pathways. Repetition makes them stronger.'[13] This ritual tells your child not only who they are, but who they're becoming.

4. Model curiosity in action

Take apart a broken appliance, start a mini garden, or try to fix something without googling the instructions. Let your child watch you get things wrong and keep trying. This visible struggle builds the foundation for perseverance and flexible thinking. Carol Dweck, known for her research on growth mindset, says, 'The view you adopt for yourself profoundly affects the way you lead your life.'[14] Showing children that curiosity is an ongoing journey, not a finished product, helps wire their brains for adaptive, resilient learning.

5. Join a club or team together

Choose a weekly shared physical activity, such as cycling around the oval, learning to swim, or even indoor rock climbing. These rhythmic movements release dopamine, reduce stress and build stronger emotional regulation when done in trusted company. In *Spark: The Revolutionary New Science of Exercise and the Brain*, psychiatrist John Ratey explains, 'Exercise

is the single most powerful tool you have to optimise brain function.'[15] Doing it side by side makes it even more effective.

THE BENEFITS FOR OUR CHILDREN

I'm sure we can all agree by this point in the book that every skill we call '21st century' rests on the foundation of a healthy mind. Communication, collaboration, empathy, creativity and critical thinking all fall apart if a child is tired, anxious or overstimulated. When screens take over, sleep is interrupted, focus becomes scattered and emotions feel harder to manage. But when we find balance, we create the conditions for these skills to grow naturally.

And when children sleep well and move their bodies regularly, they can concentrate for longer, listen more deeply and approach challenges with greater flexibility. A recent study from the University of South Australia found that any kind of movement, even something gentle like walking or Tai Chi, can boost brain function and memory in children and adults.[16] Another large review published earlier this year showed that exercise improves thinking skills and memory across all ages, with the strongest benefits seen in children and teenagers.[17]

And it is not just the brain that benefits. When children

spend less time scrolling and more time connecting face-to-face, they begin to develop empathy, emotional intelligence and the confidence to share their ideas with clarity. One study published in the *Journal of Academic Medicine* found that children with lower screen time demonstrated higher levels of cooperation, empathy and self-control compared to those who used screens more heavily.[18] By 'practising the pause', reflecting, and learning to manage their feelings, rather than rushing from one digital distraction to the next, they build resilience that stays with them in classrooms, on sports fields and eventually in their adult lives.

And so, reducing screen time and protecting mental well-being is not only about preventing harm, it's about opening the door to a richer and more balanced childhood. The ability to think critically, to collaborate with others, to lead with compassion and to create with imagination all begin with a mind that is rested, steady and strong. When we give children the right conditions in which to thrive, the results are immediate, they endure and they shape the adults our children will one day become. Below are some of the ways they stand to flourish.

Deeper sense of purpose and motivation

When children engage in meaningful, hands-on activities, like helping in the garden, solving real-life problems or contributing to the family, they begin to understand that their actions matter. They see the effects of their efforts and start to ask, 'How can I help?' This sense of purpose nurtures intrinsic motivation and a desire to contribute, not just achieve.

Sharper focus and attention

When children practise tuning into real-world tasks, like following a recipe, finishing a puzzle or building something by hand, they're strengthening the brain's ability to focus. In a world full of distractions, this quiet skill becomes a superpower. It teaches them how to be present, finish what they start and stay engaged even when things get tricky.

Greater resilience

True resilience isn't built by shielding children from difficulty, it's built by helping them face it. Whether it's fixing a mistake, handling a disagreement or persevering through a tough moment, these challenges stretch their inner strength. Each time they fall and get back up, they're wiring their brains for courage, confidence and long-term adaptability.

Stronger emotional regulation

Brains that are well-rested, well-nourished and not constantly overstimulated are better equipped to manage big feelings. Children begin to recognise when they're nearing overwhelm and learn how to pause, breathe and respond, rather than react. This kind of emotional self-awareness lays the groundwork for thoughtful decision-making and strong relationships.

Lifelong healthier habits

When sleep, movement, connection and rest are part of the family rhythm, children grow up knowing how to take care of their minds. These habits become second nature, something they return to, even as life gets busy. Over time, they don't just know what keeps them well; they live it, carrying those skills into adulthood with confidence.

IN SUMMARY

The future is not asking our children to memorise more, it's asking them to *be more*. More present. More balanced. More human.

The most important skills for tomorrow – resilience, empathy, adaptability and curiosity – cannot be downloaded, memorised or ticked off a checklist. They cannot be taught in the traditional sense. They must be *lived*. Felt. Practised in the real world, through real relationships, real challenges and real wonder.

A child does not learn compassion by reading about it. They learn it by helping a neighbour, comforting a friend, or being gently guided by an adult who models kindness in everyday moments. Creativity is not sparked by endless worksheets, it is born from boredom, exploration and permission to make a mess. True confidence doesn't come from praise alone, but from facing difficulty, trying again and discovering their own strength.

As families, we hold the power to create these experiences. Not through pressure, but through presence. Not through perfection, but through rhythm, intention and love.

We are not just raising students, we are raising citizens, leaders, thinkers and carers of tomorrow's world. That kind of work doesn't happen in a rush of activities or pressure to perform. It happens slowly, quietly, in the spaces in between: a consistent bedtime, a walk without a phone, a problem we solve together.

And so the question remains: *what is the most important 21st-century skill?* Well, it might just be remembering what makes us human and protecting it, together.

CHAPTER 9

What is artificial intelligence (AI) and why all the fuss?

There's a lot of buzz about AI, from wild doomsday predictions to promises of a technological paradise. The truth is, AI isn't here to take over or save the world overnight, but it is opening new doors and offering some exciting opportunities.

First, what exactly is AI? The dictionary definition of 'artificial' includes synonyms such as insincere, contrived or fake. But 'artificial' just means 'made by people' and AI is all about clever computer programs designed to help us out. If you're interested in learning more, Toby Walsh's book *Faking It* explores the ins and outs of AI.[1] What's important is that AI isn't about computers being smarter than us; it's about using technology to make everyday life a little easier and a lot more interesting.

AI tools are impressive, but they cannot replace the creativity and adaptability we bring as parents. Real intelligence is about coming up with new ideas, solving problems and growing with every experience. AI, on the other hand, is like a turbocharged assistant; it can quickly process lots of information and spot patterns, but it relies on what it's already been taught. It doesn't 'think' the way we do, and it's certainly not running the show!

Many AI systems are built on learning algorithms, a technology that's actually been around for decades. Imagine showing your child hundreds of pictures of cats and dogs and helping them label which is which. Eventually, they'll get really good at telling the difference. That's how these programs work: they learn from lots of examples, then use that knowledge to help us in practical ways.

But just as we know our children have a unique way of seeing the world, computers don't quite have our knack for understanding the unfamiliar. Show an algorithm a cup shaped like a cat and it might get confused, while our kids instantly spot it for what it is. AI doesn't have experiences, memories or feelings; it's just really good at sorting through what it's already seen.

AI has been around for quite a while. Tools like voice

assistants ('Hey Siri!' or 'Hey Google!'), navigation apps and even those friendly chatbots on websites are all powered by these algorithms. They're there to lend a hand with reminders, directions or quick answers, freeing up time for us to focus on the things that matter most, like family fun and connection.

Of course, with all this technology, it's vital for us to keep an eye on how algorithms shape our choices. The key is to remember that while AI can be a helpful guide, it's our values, creativity and love that truly lead the way. By staying curious and informed, we can make sure technology supports our families in positive, empowering ways, leaving us free to enjoy every moment, both online and off.

Picture this: you're standing in the kitchen, hands full of laundry, and your kid looks up at you with big, hopeful eyes. 'Water or orange juice?' you ask, trying your best to sound like you're offering real options (but knowing, deep down, there's no way you're cleaning up a milkshake explosion today). Sound familiar? Welcome to the world of choices, where, as parents, we give the options, but we're quietly curating the menu.

Let's talk about us adults. We like to think we're in charge, right? That we have free choice. You decided to read this book, even though you could have been answering emails, folding laundry, scrolling on your phone or finally hiding that toy that's been chirping for days. When you're ready, you'll stop reading and move on to something else. Because you choose to do so, right?

But do you truly decide what you are going to do at any given instant? There are restrictions such as the law and the need to earn a living, but within those boundaries, you generally choose. This is the mark of a free society. Each individual gets to decide where they live, who they hang out with and what they do on their day off.

But here's the thing: philosophers have been arguing for centuries about whether we *really* have free will. Some say every decision you make today is just a domino falling from a decision you made yesterday (or last year, or the night you thought rum shots were a good idea). Maybe now, if someone offers you rum or vodka, your past experience with the porcelain throne will nudge your decision toward vodka. Or even water. That's not fate, it's just you learning the hard way. It suggests that all our choices are just a trail of yesterday's decisions leading us by the nose. We don't decide anything in isolation.

Whether you're 'Team Free Will' or 'Team Pre-Programmed', here's something we can agree on: being able to make choices feels pretty exciting. Babies start with about two options: eat or sleep. As they grow, their options balloon: slide or swing, apple or banana, socks or no socks. And what do kids want most? To make their own choices! 'But I want a milkshake!' Sound familiar?

So what does all this have to do with smartphones, AI and that endless parade of 'helpful' suggestions? Well, here's the twist: every time we hand over our decisions to our devices, we're trading in a little bit of our choice-making power.

Maybe you're thinking, 'No way, my phone gives me access to the world! I can video call anyone, get the news before it's news, and I have more "friends" than my kid has Labubus!' Sure, that's the pitch. But let's peek behind the curtain.

When you search online for a gym, do you get every gym in your area? Nope. You get the ones the search engine thinks you'll want to see; often the ones that paid for the privilege. The photos and the reviews are carefully handpicked to nudge you into 'choosing'. It's like offering your toddler carrot sticks or apple slices and pretending the cookie jar doesn't even exist.

Social media is even sneakier. Facebook, Instagram, TikTok and all the other platforms use clever algorithms to decide what pops up in your feed. They track what you click and what you like, and serve up more of the same. Click on cute puppy videos? Suddenly, it's all puppies, all the time. Like one post about unicorn cakes? You're in for a glittery ride. It's not that you don't have choices; it's just that your choices are being selected for you, just like you do for your kids.

So are we really choosing, or are we just picking between 'water' and 'orange juice' when what we really want is ice cream? Sometimes the most important choices are the ones missing from the menu, and we may not even notice they're gone. Next time your phone gives you three options, ask yourself: 'Are these *all* the options? Or just the ones the algorithm wants me to see?' Odds are, there's a cookie jar hiding somewhere.

This matters because it's part of why we're seeing more folks huddling at opposite ends of the playground; 'Team Left' or 'Team Right', no mixing allowed. Algorithms feed you what you like and before you know it, it seems like everyone agrees with you. Click on a post supporting one side and you'll get a flood of similar posts, never seeing the other side of the story. It's a recipe for a one-note echo chamber and honestly, it doesn't make play dates any more peaceful.

'But wait,' you say, 'that just helps me find what I want faster. It's helping me to narrow down the search to what is important to me.' True, but here's the next question: why these options? Or why are the options I *don't* see not being offered? Who's picking what you see (and what you don't)? Remember, these apps are built by huge multinational companies whose main goal is to keep you online and make a profit. That should immediately be a red flag that what you are being shown might not be in your best interests . . . but is likely to be in theirs. It's definitely not helping you find the best snack for your kid's lunchbox. That's your job!

And here's the kicker: AI and algorithms don't think or have ethics or morals. They don't care about right or wrong; they just chase clicks, likes and whatever keeps us scrolling. ChatGPT had to be hard-coded before its release to not be sexist and racist, because it uses training material from everything on the internet, and we can only imagine what it might learn from!

AI is not a critical thinker; it will fall into traps like reporting conspiracy theories as factual because they are prevalent on the internet. It treats all information as equal. If you allow a learning algorithm such as ChatGPT to just run without specific guidelines, it quickly becomes the worst of the internet and creates content based on that misinformation. In fact, the geniuses at Facebook have claimed that they have no idea what the Facebook algorithms use as criteria to determine what people see, just that they're very good at keeping people scrolling.

Even worse, these algorithms are being used to target us and our kids. It was recently shown that when a young girl deletes an Instagram post of herself, within a second, faster than the Flash, her feed will be full of cosmetic ads. Instagram knows she is feeling bad about how she looks, so it is a great time to convince her she needs a new lipstick or facial peel. This is targeted advertising to take advantage of our kids when they're feeling vulnerable.

But don't panic! AI can do some amazing things, like spotting problems in medical scans, helping design new medicines, or making sure no one accidentally packs a toy dinosaur in their carry-on. In these cases, AI doesn't replace real people, it just helps them do their jobs better. It's like having an extra set of hands at the grocery store (if only, right?).

What we need to be aware of is that AI systems are not really 'intelligent'. They are designed to *look* intelligent. They have no moral or ethical compass and they will use whatever works to solve the problem. When used on social media, they limit our choices and make us more divided. There are some great aspects of AI that can improve human performance, but they cannot replace it.

So the next time you're offered a choice by your phone, remember: you're being parented by the algorithm. Don't be afraid to peek in the cookie jar and see what other options are out there. After all, as parents, we know that sometimes the best choices are the ones we make for ourselves, and every now and then, the ones no algorithm could ever predict.

HYPE VS REALITY – DEMYSTIFYING AI

The moment we teach a machine to sound like us is also the moment we must ask: what makes *our* voices truly matter?

Artificial intelligence is no longer something down the road, it's already here, embedded in the background of everyday life. It writes our messages, corrects our spelling, curates our feeds, suggests what we might want to say, eat, hear or buy. Quietly and relentlessly, it speeds things up, smooths things over and removes friction from our days. It's clever, yes. Convenient, definitely. But it is not *alive*.

Our children aren't watching AI emerge, they're growing up within its web. For them, it's normal for a camera to enhance their smile before they've even seen the photo. Normal for answers to appear before questions are fully asked. Normal for a device to finish their sentence before they've finished thinking. But when something becomes normal, it becomes invisible. And when something is invisible, it often escapes scrutiny.

AI doesn't have to be conscious to change our lives. It's not plotting to replace us, but it is reshaping us. Not through control, but through constant ease. And ease, though tempting, can quietly dull the very qualities that define us as human: curiosity, perseverance, empathy and imagination.

A machine can mimic creativity, but it cannot feel the

rush of inspiration. It can write a poem, but it can't feel heartbreak. It can offer facts, but it can't hold your hand in silence when the facts aren't enough. It can generate, predict and calculate, but it cannot *care*. And that's not a failing of AI, it's a reminder of what makes human beings extraordinary.

Increasingly, we are forgetting this. In classrooms and living rooms, children are being taught to use AI, but not always to question it. A 2023 OECD report found that while over 60 per cent of students now rely on generative AI for their assignments, only a fraction have been shown how to evaluate its suggestions or check for bias.[2] Meanwhile, studies like Canada's MediaSmarts report that nearly half of all children believe AI is more reliable than their teachers. That's not just a misunderstanding, that's a moment of truth.[3]

If we let the line blur between imitation and insight, we may raise a generation fluent in producing answers but unpractised in *living the questions*. And that's where the real danger lies; not in the technology itself, but in what we choose to surrender to it.

This chapter isn't intended to spark fear, it's meant to rekindle awareness. To remind us that when we outsource too much, we can lose sight of what it means to create, connect and become. That struggle you feel when you try to explain a hard idea in your own words? That's learning. That pause between thoughts? That's reflection. That awkward silence between friends? That's real. And it matters. The risk is not that AI will feel too much like us. The risk is that we might stop acting like ourselves.

Friendship is often messy. Understanding takes time. Forgiveness requires humility. And the most important human experiences – love, trust, joy and loss – don't run on data. They unfold slowly. They involve risk. They demand presence.

One day, a child will ask not just how AI works, but what it means to be human in a world where machines do so much. When that question comes, we won't need a technical explanation. We'll need a story. A story about trying again. About listening deeply. About making something new, not because it was easy, but because it mattered.

AI might help build the future, but it cannot *feel* it. It cannot *dream* it. It cannot love, forgive or wonder. Those are our superpowers and they'll always be ours, if we're brave enough to keep using them.

So let's not measure our worth by how efficiently we keep up with the machines. Let's measure it by how bravely we remain human in a world that forgets to slow down. Let's remind our children that while AI may offer speed, precision and endless output, only humans can offer presence, meaning and heart. In the end, it won't be the machines that define our future, it will be the choices we make, the values we hold and the courage we have to keep feeling, wondering and creating anyway. That is, and will always be, our greatest strength.

THE BENEFITS OF UNPLUGGING FROM AI

When we begin to outsource our thinking to AI, we don't just hand over tasks, we risk handing over the very process of discovery. Artificial intelligence can generate ideas, write stories, even solve problems. But when we rely on it too often, we dull the part of our brain responsible for original thought. Creativity is not born from convenience, it grows out of curiosity, uncertainty and the willingness to try, fail and try again. By stepping away from AI-generated solutions, we give our minds the space to stretch, wonder and make unexpected connections. That's where *real* innovation lives.

AI also has a way of fragmenting our attention. The more it predicts what we want and fills in the blanks, the less we need to concentrate, follow through, or stay with a challenge. This has consequences. When children are constantly fed ideas, conclusions or quick fixes by a machine, they miss out on the cognitive workout that builds memory, deep focus and sustained attention. Stepping back from AI allows the brain to re-engage in the full process of learning; not just absorbing outcomes, but wrestling with the steps that led there.

Most importantly, unplugging from AI helps children reconnect with their own inner compass. AI tools don't just assist, they *influence*. They shape language, aesthetics, decision-making and, over time, identity. If a child leans too heavily on AI to express themselves, they may start to doubt the value of their own voice. But when we create space away from those tools, children rediscover their instincts, their preferences and their quirks. They become authors of their own thoughts, not just editors of something pre-generated.

In the end, the most human parts of us – curiosity, grit, empathy and imagination – are not programmable. They are developed slowly, through lived experience. AI may be able to predict what we'll type next, but it cannot replace the wonder of thinking for ourselves. And that is the greatest reason to unplug; not to reject technology, but to remember what it means to be truly alive and fully engaged with our own mind.

THOUGHT-PROVOKING STATS

Children exposed to high levels of AI-curated content are 45 per cent more likely to struggle with attention and impulse control, compared to those with lower digital exposure.[4]

Based on a 2022 Slovakian study, researchers found that 41 per cent of teenagers could not distinguish between true and fake online health messages.[5]

Children and adolescents who spend four or more hours a day on screens have approximately 65 per cent higher odds of experiencing depressive symptoms and 45 per cent higher odds of anxiety, compared to those with lower screen time.[6]

Only one in five parents feels confident that they understand how AI shapes what their child sees online, leaving most families unprepared to guide responsible use.[7]

Thirty-three per cent of teens now use AI companions such as ChatGPT, Character.AI or Replika for emotional support, conversation and even romantic interaction.[8]

We don't need to look far to see the effects; these numbers paint a clear picture. Artificial intelligence is no longer just something to be curious about; it's something our children are already living with, every single day. From the content they consume to the choices they believe are theirs, AI quietly nudges their thinking, habits and beliefs.

This makes our role as parents and caregivers more important than ever. Understanding and actively managing AI exposure isn't just good parenting, it's essential. If we want our children to grow up with the ability to focus deeply, think critically and stay emotionally grounded, we must offer them something AI can't: perspective, wisdom and human connection.

We do this not by rejecting technology, but by reminding our children that real thinking takes time. That it's okay not to have instant answers. That curiosity is more powerful than convenience. And that mistakes are not a glitch; they're part of learning.

AI will continue to advance. But our children's humanity, their ability to reflect, question and care, will always be their greatest strength. Let's make sure they never forget that.

Our children are increasingly leaning on AI tools for their speed and convenience. And while efficiency has its place, the easiest way is not always the best. Sometimes, it's the long road, the one that gives us grazed knees, windswept hair and dirty fingernails that leaves the deepest imprint. It's in the stumbles, the missteps and the honest effort that true growth is forged. AI will always be there with a neat, polished answer. But it's not the soft-spoken compliments or easy wins that build character; it's the hard truths, the uncomfortable moments and the quiet perseverance that shape who we become.

Even though an AI bot will often tell you exactly what you want to hear, it's those moments of tension, doubt and struggle, the ones where nothing comes easily, that teach us the most. And while machines might guide us through tasks, they'll never guide us through becoming.

In a world that's changing faster than ever, we must remind our children that shortcuts don't build resilience. Doing the hard thing, even when a bot offers an easier path, is often what prepares us for the real challenges ahead.

WHAT CAN PARENTS DO?

1. Weekend insect hunt and sketch

Head outdoors with just a notebook and pencils to the garden, a local park or along a bush trail, and observe the tiny world beneath your feet. Gently sketch any insects you see, paying attention to shape, movement and colour. When you get home, use old encyclopedias or field guides to identify the species together. The magic lies in close observation and quiet discovery. As author Rachel Carson reminds us, 'Those who dwell among the beauties and mysteries of the earth are never alone or weary of life.'[9]

2. Create a polaroid photo journal

Use an old polaroid or film camera to take one meaningful photo each day; something curious, beautiful or personal. In a scrapbook, each child can write a short reflection beneath their photo, capturing not just what they saw, but how it made them feel. Over time, it becomes a visual diary full of thought and intention. As photographer and journalist Dorothea Lange once said, 'Photography takes an instant out of time, altering life by holding it still.'[10]

3. Daily family journalling

Gather around the table each evening, no devices, just pencils and paper, and write together. Children might jot down something they're grateful for, a moment that challenged them, or what they hope for tomorrow. It doesn't need to be perfect; it just needs to be theirs. The French writer Voltaire captured this beautifully, 'Writing is the painting of the voice.'[11] In a world full of predictive text, this simple ritual reconnects us to our own thoughts.

4. Weekly screen-time check-in

Every Sunday evening, sit down as a family and look at everyone's screen-time totals. Use a simple paper chart and ask open-ended questions like, 'How did that feel?' or 'What might we try next week?' Make it fun: whoever used

screens the least picks the next family activity. This exercise is about awareness, not blame. As management consultant Peter Drucker wrote, 'What gets measured gets managed.'[12] This builds accountability, mindfulness and a bit of friendly competition.

5. Restore something together

Find an old bike, a billy cart, or a bit of discarded furniture and bring it back to life. Sand it, paint it, tighten the bolts and test it out. Let your child take the lead when they can and celebrate the result together. This sort of activity is hands-on, messy and can instil pride. As Benjamin Franklin's timeless wisdom reminds us, 'Tell me and I forget, teach me and I remember, involve me and I learn.'[13]

THE BENEFITS FOR OUR CHILDREN

From the first time we used fire to cook our food, to the discovery of the wheel, and later the agricultural revolution, every tool humans have ever created has changed us in some way. Yes, artificial intelligence can be clever, quick and helpful, but it cannot teach children how to wonder, how to wrestle with a problem, or how to trust their own ideas. If our children rely on it too much, they risk missing out on the qualities that matter most in life: creativity, resilience, empathy and critical thinking. That is why making space to step back is so important. It gives those qualities room to grow. And we need to remember this for ourselves too. As adults, we are just as tempted by shortcuts and easy answers, and just as likely to let our imagination fade if we are not careful.

When children unplug from AI and figure things out on their own, something powerful happens. Their focus sharpens, their memory deepens and they learn to stay with a challenge instead of skipping straight to the quick fix. When they use their own words, sketches or ideas instead of a machine, they begin to trust their voice and see that their perspective matters. And when they try, stumble and try again, they discover that resilience is not built on convenience, it is built on effort and persistence. Research supports this: children who engage more in unstructured, self-directed activities develop stronger executive function and problem-solving skills than those who rely heavily on digital tools.[14]

Limiting our dependence on AI is not about rejecting technology. It's about protecting what matters most. The ability to think independently, to work well with others, to show compassion and to imagine something new all begin with a mind that is fully engaged, not distracted by shortcuts. And when we give children, and ourselves, the right conditions to thrive, the benefits are immediate and lasting. Below are some of the ways children flourish when they are encouraged to grow as thinkers, creators and problem-solvers in their own right.

Improved cognitive control and confidence

When children take regular breaks from relying on AI and work through things on their own – whether it's solving a tricky problem or finishing a creative task – they build focus, memory and the ability to shift gears when needed. These small moments of self-direction slowly grow into something bigger: a quiet confidence that says, 'I can figure this out without being told.'

Greater emotional resilience

Stepping back from screens, even for short periods, helps children tune into how they're really feeling. They begin to recognise what makes them feel calm, overwhelmed, excited or tired. Over time, this emotional awareness becomes their internal toolkit, helping them handle stress, regulate mood and settle into deeper, more restful sleep.

Richer social bonds

When families talk openly about how technology works, laugh at real-life stories, or problem-solve side by side, something special happens: connection deepens. Children learn to listen more carefully, express themselves clearly and respond with empathy. These shared human moments strengthen the relationships that truly nourish them.

Heightened creativity and independent thinking

Without constant nudges from AI about what to say, draw, write or even wear, children start thinking for themselves. Their imagination stretches, they take risks and they bounce ideas off siblings and friends. This kind of free, unstructured creativity is where innovation is born and where children learn to trust their own voices.

A balanced lifelong relationship with AI

When children grow up learning how to use AI rather than simply relying on it, they begin to see it for what it truly is: a tool, not a teacher. By encouraging moments of real thinking, creativity and problem-solving without AI's constant suggestions, we help them build the habits of discernment, curiosity and independence. Over time, they learn that just because something is easy or instant doesn't mean it's better. And that their own ideas, however imperfect or slow to form, are often far more powerful.

IN SUMMARY

AI isn't the enemy, but it's not the answer to everything either. Yes, it's remarkable. It's transforming medicine, powering clean energy and solving complex equations in seconds. But let's not forget, *we* made it what it is. AI is only ever a reflection of what humans feed into it.

In the right hands, it's a powerful tool for solving problems, building connections and driving progress. But if we're not careful, if we stop paying attention, it will erode something far more precious: our children's ability to think for themselves, to imagine freely and to solve problems the long way round.

By speaking honestly about how AI works, encouraging questions and carving out time for real-world learning, we offer something AI never can: human depth. Empathy, curiosity, integrity and imagination aren't optional extras. They are the very qualities that set us apart.

And the future? Well, it won't belong to those who always choose the quickest route or accept every automated answer. It will be shaped by those who can think for themselves, who can sit with uncertainty and who value being human above being efficient. Our role is to make sure those people are our children.

A final word

Technology is like a powerful river. When channelled with care and intention, it can irrigate fields, bring life to communities and connect distant lands. But if controlled by the few or left unchecked, it can flood the whole landscape, eroding our very foundations.

Throughout this book, we have sought to illuminate a simple truth: technology isn't the villain. It's more like the helpful sidekick that sometimes gets it wrong. Ever since our ancestors first knocked two rocks together, we've been inventing tools to make life easier, and today's tech is just the latest chapter in a very long story. From fire to FaceTime, it's always been there to lend a hand.

Used with care and intention, it can be extraordinary. In the past, it gave us fire, allowed us to make tools and helped us travel thousands of kilometres across land and sea. Today, it connects us across continents, sparks ideas we never thought possible, and even helps us find cures for diseases that would once have taken millennia to cure.

But the hard truth is that no matter how extraordinary technology may be, it cannot do the work of being human. It cannot replace the look in a parent's eyes, the goodnight hug, the encouragement of a teacher, or the laughter shared between friends. These are the things that sustain us, shape our sense of belonging and remind us of what really matters.

Think back to your own childhood. The afternoons outside, the games you made up, the belly laughs, the scraped knees, the hours that passed without a single screen in sight. Those messy, joyful moments were not just entertainment, they were the foundations of imagination, resilience and connection. And the truth is, we need those same ingredients today. No piece of technology, no matter how advanced, can ever replace the grounding power of real human connection and the memories created along the way. And guess what? Our kids need all of that just as much as we did.

As the American philosopher and psychologist John Dewey once said, 'Education is not preparation for life; education is life itself.'[1] And life, in its fullness, is not a never-ending scroll of notifications. Life is found in curiosity, creativity, presence and relationships. It is found in the quiet of reflection, in the warmth of eye contact, in a hand held tightly, in a conversation that drifts and deepens without distraction. And despite what we all may think, life involves boredom! It's actually essential, even though it sometimes feels uncomfortable, because it sparks imagination beyond belief and allows new thoughts to emerge.

This is not to say technology has no role in our lives. Far from it. It can help us learn, collaborate and stay connected. But there's a tipping point: when devices become the boss instead of the assistant, we lose focus, feel less connected and miss out on those hilarious, spontaneous family moments.

That is why the heart of this book is not about rejecting technology, but about reclaiming presence and rediscovering what truly matters. It is about creating space and prioritising the qualities that make us uniquely human; about choosing to live as though our relationships, not our devices, are the first things we reach for in the morning and the final comfort we seek before sleep.

The goal is to notice when technology serves us well and to recognise when it's taking more than it should. Our families, schools, workplaces and communities should be places where technology supports, but never replaces, the essence of our humanity. That essence is found in our capacity for connection, empathy and understanding. We are, after all, the 'connected species', and when we choose to collaborate, communicate and compromise with one another, we thrive on every level – spiritually, intellectually, emotionally and socially.

LOOKING AHEAD

When we picture the future, it's easy to imagine that someone else is in control and that we can simply opt in or out as new things appear. That is partly true, but *only* if we remain aware. The reality is that the future rests in our hands. Thirty years ago, a bus or train carriage would be filled with conversation, laughter and the sense of being together. Today, on almost any form of public transport, you will see heads bowed, earphones in and faces lit by blue light. The only sound will be the rattle of the rails or the hum of the traffic.

We must decide what kind of future we want. The next generation will not be shaped by the words we speak, but by the way we live alongside them – day after day, moment by moment. Children and young people are observing us more closely than we realise. They are learning not just from our advice, but from our habits, our priorities and the choices we make.

There is no question that technology will keep evolving. New platforms, new devices and new ways of connecting will appear faster than we can predict or fully understand. We don't yet know what the digital landscape will look like in ten or twenty years' time, but one thing is certain: our response to it now matters. Our role is not to resist change blindly or to reject technology altogether. It is to place it where it belongs, behind the deeper human needs of connection, creativity, compassion and presence.

When we do this, something powerful emerges. Children will not merely survive the digital age; they will flourish within it. They will grow into adults who see technology as a tool, not a crutch they cannot walk without. We are nurturing future citizens who know that genuine connection is found not in likes or followers, but in love, kindness and friendship. Adults who can be fully present to the richness of the real world, rather than endlessly pulled away into that dim blue light.

And let's be clear: this is not just about children. It is about us as parents and caregivers too. The lives we live today, the choices we make to pause, to connect and to step away from the screen all shape not only our kids' futures, but the quality of our own lives. As we model positive behaviours and healthy habits around technology, we do more than guide our kids, we enrich ourselves. In choosing presence, balance and a mindful use of technology, we nourish our own existence with greater connection, wellbeing, health and restoration. If we want the next generation to flourish, we must show them, through the way *we* live, what it means to remain grounded, balanced and fully human in the digital age.

THE SEVEN GOLDEN PRINCIPLES

As we near the end of this book, here are seven principles that, if adhered to and adopted into your lifestyle and culture, will massively help with the wellbeing and connection of your home, school and workplace.

1. Model the behaviour you want to see

Children (and those around us) notice what we do far more than what we say. If they see us putting the phone aside, choosing conversation over scrolling, or showing curiosity about the world beyond the screen, everyone's wellbeing will improve. If you put your phone down for a chat or a game, they'll notice, and maybe even follow!

2. Create tech-free times and spaces

Homes and schools thrive on rituals that prioritise connection. Meals without devices, bedrooms kept for rest and family gatherings free from distraction remind us all of what matters most. These small boundaries soon become part of the culture of a household or community.

3. Prioritise eye-to-eye over eye-to-screen

Real connection happens when we look into someone's eyes, listen closely, hold their hand and allow ourselves to be present. What we might call 'eye time' nourishes the brain and heart in ways a device never can.

4. Use technology with intention, not habit

Devices are not inherently harmful, but when they fill every empty moment, they start to steal our attention and dull our creativity. By being mindful of when and why we use our devices, we ensure technology serves us, never the other way around.

5. Encourage curiosity and imagination

The earth is an amazing place. You're on a rock floating through the universe, after all! Life beyond the screen is full of opportunities to explore, problems to solve and things to create. Whether through art, outdoor play or simple tinkering, children (and adults too) flourish when their hands and minds are engaged in the real world.

6.   Embrace boredom

Boredom is not the enemy, it is the fertile ground where imagination takes root. When children and adults are given a reprieve from constant stimulation, the mind gains the space to form new connections, and creativity has room to flourish. In the stillness of nothing to do, the brain discovers wonderful ways to make the world around us richer, more inviting and more exciting.

7.   Freedom within limits

Freedom matters, but it must always be balanced with limits. Boundaries are not about restriction; they provide the framework in which resilience, self-control and lifelong healthy habits can take root. And remember, whatever boundaries are agreed upon, they must be honoured by everyone under the same roof. Modelling the behaviour we hope to see in the children in our care is one of the most powerful lessons we can ever give.

A MESSAGE OF HOPE

We know that there's a lot to take in, but as we've said from the beginning, you are not alone in this. None of us has all the answers and the truth is we are all learning as we go. Technology is moving so quickly that it can feel almost impossible to keep up. At times it's overwhelming. Yet here's the hopeful part: we *do* have choices. Every day, in the small and ordinary moments, we can decide how technology shapes our lives. Some of those choices will help us to flourish. Others may quietly hold us back. What matters most is not perfection, but awareness and the willingness to keep showing up and living a life where we value connection over entertainment.

There will always be times when screens slip in as a band-aid or a moment's rest. Perhaps you're tired and just need twenty quiet minutes. The kids end up with a game or a video. That isn't failure. That's life. It only becomes a problem when those moments stop being the exception and gradually become the rule. That is a shift we can notice and one we have the power to change.

The challenges are real, but the rewards are far greater. Raising kids who can thrive both offline and online is worth the effort. When they learn to use technology wisely, they don't just perform better at school. They safeguard their mental health. They build resilience. They grow into thoughtful, creative and deeply connected human beings. The kind of adults the world urgently needs. And along the way, we too rediscover balance, connection and presence in our own lives.

So if anything has resonated with you in this book, our hope is that you choose presence, even when it feels inconvenient. We hope you practise balance, even when it takes discipline. And we hope you trust that those small, daily decisions – looking up, listening fully, putting the phone aside, or inviting connection – are shaping not only our children's futures, but also the quality of our own lives.

It is never too late to reset. Never too late to pause, to change course, to begin again. Each day offers an opportunity to start anew with deeper understanding and clearer intentions towards a better today and an even brighter tomorrow.

That new beginning starts right here.

Select bibliography

Australian Institute of Family Studies. (2015). Children's Screen Time: Longitudinal Study of Australian Children. Canberra: Australian Government.

Baldwin, J. (1972). *No Name in the Street.* New York: Dial Press.

Beard, J. (1974). *Beard on Food: The Best Recipes and Kitchen Wisdom from the Dean of American Cooking.* New York: Alfred A. Knopf.

Breuning, L.G. (2016). *The Science of Positivity: Stop Negative Thought Patterns by Changing Your Brain Chemistry.* New York: Simon & Schuster.

Brown, B. (2010). *The Gifts of Imperfection: Let Go of Who You Think You're Supposed to Be and Embrace Who You Are.* Center City, Minnesota: Hazelden Publishing.

Brown, B. (2018). *Dare to Lead: Brave Work. Tough Conversations. Whole Hearts*. New York: Random House.

Carson, R. (1965). *The Sense of Wonder*. New York: Harper & Row.

Clear, J. (2018). *Atomic Habits: An Easy & Proven Way to Build Good Habits & Break Bad Ones*. New York: Avery Publishing.

Csikszentmihalyi, M. (1990). *Flow: The Psychology of Optimal Experience*. London: HarperCollins.

Donaldson, O.F. (1993). *Playing by Heart: The Vision and Practice of Belonging*. New York: Running Press.

Drucker, P.F. (1999). *Management Challenges for the 21st Century*. New York: HarperBusiness.

Dweck, C.S. (2006). *Mindset: The New Psychology of Success*. New York: Random House.

Einstein, A. (n.d.). As quoted in Calaprice, A. (2000). *The Expanded Quotable Einstein*. Princeton University Press.

Einstein, A. (2009). *Cosmic Religion: With Other Opinions and Aphorisms*. New York: Dover Publications.

Elliot, J. (1978). *The Journals of Jim Elliot*. Ada, Michigan: Fleming H. Revell Company.

Emerson, R.W. (1875). *Letters and Social Aims*. Boston: James R. Osgood & Co.

Harari, Y.N. (2018). *21 Lessons for the 21st Century*. New York: Spiegel & Grau.

Hitchcock, E. (1790). *Memoirs of the Bloomsgrove Family*. Boston: Thomas and Andrews.

Jamison, K.R. (2004). *Exuberance: The Passion for Life*. New York: Alfred A. Knopf.

Kabat-Zinn, J. (1994). *Wherever You Go, There You Are: Mindfulness Meditation in Everyday Life*. New York: Hyperion.
Keller, H. (1903). *The Story of My Life*. New York: Doubleday.

Lamott, A. (2012). *Help, Thanks, Wow: The Three Essential Prayers*. New York: Riverhead Books.
Louv, R. (2008). *Last Child in the Woods: Saving Our Children from Nature-Deficit Disorder*. New York: Algonquin Books.
Louv, R. (2011). *The Nature Principle*. New York: Algonquin Books.

Martin, G.R.R. (2011). *A Dance with Dragons*. New York: Bantam Books.
McGinley, P. (1968). *Collected Poems*. New York: Lippincott Williams & Wilkins.
McLuhan, M. (1964). *Understanding Media: The Extensions of Man*. New York: McGraw-Hill.
Miller, S. (1803). *A Brief Retrospect of the Eighteenth Century*. Vol. 1. New York: T. and J. Swords.
Montessori, M. (1967). *The Absorbent Mind*. New York: Holt, Rinehart and Winston.
Muir, J. (1981). *Our National Parks*. University of Wisconsin Press.

Oliver, M. (2009). *Red Bird: Poems*. Boston: Beacon Press. (Poem: 'Sometimes')

Pascal, B. (1669). *Pensées*. Paris: Alphonse Lemerre.

Perry, B.D., Szalavitz, M. (2006). *The Boy Who Was Raised as a Dog: And Other Stories from a Child Psychiatrist's Notebook*. New York: Basic Books.

Picasso, P. (n.d.). As quoted in Richardson, J. (1991). *A Life of Picasso*. New York: Random House.

Ratey, J.J. (2008). *Spark: The Revolutionary New Science of Exercise and the Brain*. New York: Little, Brown.

Rohn, J. (1985). *Seven Strategies for Wealth and Happiness*. Los Angeles: Prima Publishing.

Rogers, R. Paraphrased from interviews and writings collected in Hollingsworth, A. *The Simple Faith of Mister Rogers*. (2005). New York: Thomas Nelson.

Roosevelt, R. As quoted in *Good Citizenship: The Purpose of Education*. (1940). New York: Wiley.

Santayana, G. (1981) As quoted in *The Life of Reason*. New York: Scribner.

Thoreau, H.D. (1863). *Journals of Henry David Thoreau*. New York: Houghton Mifflin.

Tutu, T. (1999). *No Future Without Forgiveness*. New York: Doubleday.

Twenge, J.M. (2017). *iGen: Why Today's Super-Connected Kids Are Growing Up Less Rebellious, More Tolerant, Less Happy and Completely Unprepared for Adulthood*. New York: Atria Books.

Twenge, J.M. (2024). *Generations: The Real Differences Between Gen Z, Millennials, Gen X, Boomers, and Silents, and What They Mean for America's Future*. New York: Atria Books.

Vallor, S. (2016). *Technology and the Virtues: A Philosophical Guide to a Future Worth Wanting.* Oxford University Press.

Voltaire. (1824). *A Philosophical Dictionary* (Vol. 1). London: Printed for J. and H.L. Hunt.

Walker, M. (2017). *Why We Sleep: Unlocking the Power of Sleep and Dreams.* New York: Scribner.

Walsch, N.D. (1995). *Conversations with God.* New York: Penguin.

Walsh, T. (2024). *Faking It: Artificial Intelligence in a Human World.* Melbourne: Black Inc.

Weil, S. (1942). *Gravity and Grace.* London: Routledge.

Williams, M.A. (2024). *The Connected Species: How Understanding the Evolution of the Human Brain Can Help You Re-connect with the World.* Woodslane Press, Sydney.

Woolf, V. (1929). *A Room of One's Own.* London: Hogarth Press.

Endnotes

Chapter 1

1 Miller, S. (1803). *A Brief Retrospect of the Eighteenth Century.* Vol. 1. New York: T. and J. Swords. p. 373.
2 Hitchcock, E. (1790). *Memoirs of the Bloomsgrove Family.* Providence: J. Carter. p. 188.
3 www.humanetech.com
4 https://bullyingfree.nz/about-bullying/lgbtqia/
5 Friendship, Loneliness, and Snapchat: An Interview with Dana Kerford, https://www.arc.unsw.edu.au/blitz/read/friendship-loneliness-and-social-media-an-interview-with-dana-kerford; https://www.projectrockit.com.au/

6   Twenge, J.M., Haidt, J., Blake, A.B., McAllister, C., Lemon, H., Le Roy, A. (2021). Worldwide increases in adolescent loneliness, *J Adolesc*. 2021 Dec; 93:257–269. doi: 10.1016/j. adolescence.2021.06.006. Epub 2021 Jul 20. PMID: 34294429

7   Gostick, A. (2023). Harvard Research Reveals The #1 Key To Living Longer And Happier. *Forbes*. https://www.forbes.com/sites/adriangostick/2023/08/15/harvard-research-reveals-the-1-key-to-living-longer-and-happier/

8   Farahany, N. (2023). TikTok is part of China's cognitive warfare campaign. *The Guardian*. https://www.theguardian.com/commentisfree/2023/mar/25/tiktok-china-cognitive-warfare-us-ban

9   Montessori, M. (1967). *The Absorbent Mind*. New York: Holt, Rinehart and Winston.

10   Ramachandran, V. (2025). Mirror Neurons and Imitation Learning as the Driving Force Behind the Great Leap Forward in Human Evolution. *Edge*. https://www.edge.org/conversation/vilayanur_ramachandran-mirror-neurons-and-imitation-learning-as-the-driving-force

11   McLuhan, M. (2022). Marching Backwards into the Future. https://elasticcreative.co.uk/2022/04/05/marshall-mcluhan/

12   Solly, M. (2019). Mary Oliver, a Poet Whose Simple Turns of Phrase Held Mass Appeal, Dies at 83. *Smithsonian Magazine*. https://www.smithsonianmag.com/smart-news/mary-oliver-poet-whose-simple-turns-phrase-held-mass-appeal-dies-83-180971302/

13 Twenge, J.M., Campbell, W.K. (2018). Associations between screen time and lower psychological well-being among children and adolescents: Evidence from a population-based study. *Preventive Medicine Reports*. 2018 Dec; 12:271–283. doi.org/10.1016/j.pmedr.2018.10.003. https://www.science direct.com/science/article/pii/S2211335518301827

14 Australian Institute of Family Studies. (2016). From *Growing Up in Australia: The Longitudinal Study of Australian Children, 2015*. Report. https://aifs.gov.au/research/commissioned-reports/childrens-screen-time

15 Orygen.org.au. (2025). New Data Indicates Moderation Is Key To Social Media Use For Teens. https://www.orygen. org.au/About/News-And-Events/2025/New-data-indicates-moderation-is-key-to-social-med

16 eSafety Commissioner. (2025). The online experiences of children in Australia. https://www.esafety.gov.au/research/the-online-experiences-of-children-in-australia

17 Australian Psychological Society. (2024). Australian teens trapped by social media apps as the 'like' button triggers mental health disorders. https://psychology.org.au/about-us/news-and-media/aps-in-the-media/2024/australian-teens-trapped-by-social-media-apps-as-t

18 BYU Speeches. https://speeches.byu.edu/speakers/carl-w-buehner/

19 Schnall, M. (2021). Wisdom Shared With Me By Desmond Tutu: 'We Are All Connected. What Unites Us Is Our Common Humanity.' *Forbes*. https://www.forbes.com/sites/

marianneschnall/2021/12/26/wisdom-shared-with-me-by-
desmond-tutu-we-are-all-connected-what-unites-us-is-our-
common-humanity/

20 Roosevelt, E. (1948). The Struggle for Human Rights. https://
erpapers.columbian.gwu.edu/struggle-human-rights-1948

21 Paths to Literacy. (n.d.). The Fred Rogers Approach:
The Importance of Human Connection. https://www.
pathstoliteracy.org/fred-rogers-approach-importance-
human-connection/

22 Schmich, M. (1998). Now Boarding At Any Newspaper,
Magazine Or Book. *Chicago Tribune.* 28 October 1998.

Chapter 2

1 Smith, A. (2022). Fulton J. Sheen's Lessons on Love &
the Greatest Commandment. *Catholic Exchange.*
https://catholicexchange.com/fulton-j-sheens-lessons-
on-love-the-greatest-commandment/

2 How Many Smartphones Are In The World? (2025). https://
www.bankmycell.com/blog/how-many-phones-are-in-the-world

3 Australian Communications and Media Authority (ACMA).
(2021). The Digital Lives of Younger Australians. https://
www.acma.gov.au/publications/2021-05/report/digital-lives-
younger-and-older-australians

4 Bettmann, J.E., Anstadt, G., Casselman, B. et al. (2021). Young
Adult Depression and Anxiety Linked to Social Media Use:
Assessment and Treatment. *Clin Soc Work J* 49, 368–379.
https://doi.org/10.1007/s10615-020-00752-1

5   Reviews.org. (2022). 2022 Mobile Phone Usage Statistics: How addicted are we? https://www.reviews.org/au/mobile/2022-mobile-phone-usage-statistics/

6   eSafety Commissioner. (2022). Parenting in the Digital Age: Insights into Parental Attitudes, Behaviours, and Concerns. Australian Government eSafety Research Reports. https://www.esafety.gov.au/research/parenting-digital-age

7   Montessori, M. (1967). Ibid.

8   Twenge, J.M., Martin, G.N., Spitzberg, B.H. (2019). Trends in US Adolescents' Media Use and Association with Depression, Suicide-Related Outcomes, and Suicide Rates, 2009–2017. *Journal of Abnormal Psychology.* 128(2), 119–133. https://doi.org/10.1037/abn0000410

9   Reviews.org. (2021). Aussies spend almost 17 years in a lifetime staring at their phones. https://www.reviews.org/au/mobile/aussie-screentime-in-a-lifetime/

10 Charles Sturt University. (2024). 91 per cent of Australian teens have a phone – but many are not keeping their identity and location secure. https://news.csu.edu.au/opinion/91-per-cent-of-australian-teens-have-a-phone-but-many-are-not-secure

11 University of Wollongong. (2025). Research finds parents' screen time may hinder child development. https://www.uow.edu.au/media/2025/research-finds-parents-screen-time-may-hinder-child-development.php

12 Baldwin, J. (1972). *No Name in the Street.* New York: Dial Press.

13 Keller, H. (1903). *The Story of My Life*. New York: Doubleday.

14 Csikszentmihalyi, M. (1990). *Flow: The Psychology of Optimal Experience*. London: HarperCollins.

15 Rohn, J. (1985). *Seven Strategies for Wealth and Happiness*. Los Angeles: Prima Publishing.

Chapter 3

1 Maguire, E.A., Gadian, D.G., Johnsrude, I.S., Good, C.D., Ashburner, J., Frackowiak, R.S., Frith, C.D. (2000). Navigation-related structural change in the hippocampi of taxi drivers. *Proc Natl Acad Sci USA*. 2000 Apr 11;97(8):4398–403. doi: 10.1073/pnas.070039597. PMID: 10716738; PMCID: PMC18253.

2 Dehaene, S., Pegado, F., Braga, L.W., Ventura, P., Nunes Filho, G., Jobert, A., Dehaene Lambertz, G., Kolinsky, R., Morais, J., Cohen, L. (2010). How learning to read changes the cortical networks for vision and language. *Science* 6009, 1359–1364.

3 Han, M.X., Lai, Z., Lim, S., Ong, Z.Y., Ng, V., Gabard-Durnam, L.J. et al. (2023). Associations between infant screen use, electroencephalography markers, and cognitive outcomes EC Law. *JAMA Pediatrics* 10.1001/jamapediatrics.2022.5674.

4 Hutton, J., Dudley, J., Horowitz-Kraus, T., DeWitt, T., Holland, S. (2019). Associations Between Screen-Based Media Use and Brain White Matter Integrity in Preschool-Aged Children. *JAMA Pediatrics* 10.1001/jamapediatrics. 2019.3869.

5   Richter, F. (2023). How AI will change our lives – new survey. *World Economic Forum*, 6 February 2023. https://www.weforum.org/stories/2023/02/ai-lives-ipsos-survey-technology/

6   UNICEF & Berkman Klein Center for Internet & Society. (2022). Digital experiences of children in the age of AI: Shaping AI policies that put children's rights at the centre. *UNICEF Office of Global Insight and Policy*. https://www.unicef.org/globalinsight/reports/digital-experiences-children-age-ai

7   Reviews.org. (2022). Cell Phone Usage Statistics. https://www.reviews.org/mobile/cell-phone-addiction/

8   Pew Research Center. (2023). Teens, Social Media and Technology. https://www.pewresearch.org/internet/2022/08/10/teens-social-media-and-technology-2022/

9   New York Society for the Prevention of Cruelty to Children (NYSPCC). (2023). Parent Perceptions of Internet Risks to Children. https://nyspcc.org/wp-content/uploads/2023/12/NYSPCC-Parent-Perceptions-of-Internet-Risks-to-Children-A-National-Survey-2023.pdf

10 Einstein, A. (n.d.). As quoted in Calaprice, A. (2000). *The Expanded Quotable Einstein*. Princeton University Press.

11 Franklin, B. (n.d.). Commonly attributed.

12 Donaldson, O.F. (1993). *Playing by Heart: The Vision and Practice of Belonging*. New York: Running Press.

13 Montessori, M. (1967). Ibid.

Chapter 4

1   Drouin, M., Kaiser, D., Miller, D. (2012). Phantom vibrations among undergraduates: Prevalence and associated psychological characteristics. *Computers in Human Behavior.* 28. 1490–1496. 10.1016/j.chb.2012.03.013.

2   Deloitte's 2019 global mobile consumer survey: Smartphones and the days of our lives. https://www.deloitte.com/ug/en/Industries/tmt/blogs/deloittes-2019-global-mobile-consumer-survey.html

3   Ra, C.K., Cho, J., Stone, M.D. et al. (2018). Association of Digital Media Use With Subsequent Symptoms of Attention-Deficit/Hyperactivity Disorder Among Adolescents. *JAMA.* 2018;320(3):255–263. doi:10.1001/jama.2018.8931

4   Rosen, L.D., Lim, A.F., Carrier, M.A., Cheever, N.A. (2021). An Empirical Examination of the Educational Impact of the Digital World on the Attention Span of Youth. *Educational Psychology Review*, 33(2), 453–472.

5   Statista Research Department. (2023). Daily Time Spent on Mobile Usage in Singapore. https://www.statista.com/statistics/1345898/singapore-daily-time-spent-mobile-usage/

6   Statista Research Department. (2023). Smartphone Usage by Age Group in Singapore. https://www.statista.com/statistics/1266889/singapore-smartphone-usage-by-age-group/

7   theAsianparent Insights. (2014). Device Usage: A Southeast Asia Study. https://s3-ap-southeast-1.amazonaws.com/

tap-sg-media/theAsianparent+Insights+Device+Usage+
A+Southeast+Asia+Study+November+2014.pdf

8   Santayana, G. (1981). As quoted in *The Life of Reason*. New York: Scribner.

9   Muir, J. (1981). *Our National Parks*. University of Wisconsin Press.

10 Lamott, A. (2012). *Help, Thanks, Wow: The Three Essential Prayers*. New York: Riverhead Books.

11 McGinley, P. (1968). *Collected Poems*. New York: Lippincott Williams & Wilkins.

12 Emerson, R.W. (1875). *Letters and Social Aims*. Boston: James R. Osgood & Co.

Chapter 5

1   Named after researcher James Flynn (1934–2020), the Flynn effect is the substantial and long-sustained increase in intelligence test scores that were measured in many parts of the world during the 20th century.

2   Ward, A.F., Duke, K., Gneezy, A., Bos, M.W. (2017). Brain Drain: The Mere Presence of One's Own Smartphone Reduces Available Cognitive Capacity. *Journal of the Association for Consumer Research*, 2(2), 140–154. https://www.journals.uchicago.edu/doi/full/10.1086/691462

3   Lepp, A., Barkley, J.E., Karpinski, A.C. (2015). The Relationship Between Cell Phone Use and Academic Performance in a Sample of U.S. College Students. *SAGE Open*, 5(1). https://doi.org/10.1177/2158244015573169

4   Ward, A.F., Duke, K., Gneezy, A., Bos, M.W. (2017). Loc. cit.

5   Clear, J. (2018). *Atomic Habits: An Easy & Proven Way to Build Good Habits & Break Bad Ones.* New York: Avery Publishing.

6   *The Times.* (2024) 'Concentration Crisis'.

7   Ward, A.F., Duke, K., Gneezy, A., Bos, M.W. (2017). Loc. cit.

8   *ScienceDirect.* (2020). Smartphone Use and Cognitive Performance. https://www.sciencedirect.com/science/article/pii/S0883035520303487

9   National Institutes of Health. (2022). Adolescent Brain Cognitive Development Study. https://abcdstudy.org

10 Pascal, B. (1669). *Pensées.* Paris: Alphonse Lemerre.

11 Walsch, N.D. (1995). *Conversations with God.* New York: Penguin.

Chapter 6

1   Williams, M.A. (2024). *The Connected Species: How understanding the evolution of the human brain can help you re-connect with the world.* Sydney: Woodslane Press.

2   Waldinger, R.J., Schulz, M.S. (2010). What's love got to do with it? Social functioning, perceived health, and daily happiness in married octogenarians. *Psychol Aging.* 2010 Jun;25(2): 422–31. doi: 10.1037/a0019087. PMID: 20545426; PMCID: PMC2896234.

3   Uhls, Y.T., Michikyan, M., Morris, J., Garcia, D., Small, G.S., Zgourou, E., Greenfeld, P.M. (2014). Five days at outdoor education camp without screens improves preteen skills with nonverbal emotion cues. *Computers in Human Behavior.* https://doi.org/10.1016/j.chb.2014.05.036

4 McDaniel, B.T., Radesky, J.T. (2018). Technoference: Parent Distraction With Technology and Associations With Child Behavior Problems. PMID: 28493400 PMCID: PMC5681450 DOI: 10.1111/cdev.12822

5 Przybylski, A.K., Weinstein, N. (2013). Can you connect with me now? How the presence of mobile communication technology influences face-to-face conversation quality. *Journal of Social and Personal Relationships*, 30(3), 237–246. https://doi.org/10.1177/0265407512453827

6 Australian Communications and Media Authority (ACMA). (2020). Kids and Mobiles: How Australian Children Are Using Mobile Phones. https://www.acma.gov.au/publications/2020-12/report/kids-and-mobiles-how-australian-children-are-using-mobile-phones

7 New South Wales Government. (2023). Mobile phone ban improves learning, concentration and socialisation. https://www.nsw.gov.au/media-releases/mobile-phone-ban-improves-learning-concentration-and-socialisation

8 Australian Communications and Media Authority (ACMA). (2020). Kids and Mobiles Report. https://www.acma.gov.au/publications/2020-12/report/kids-and-mobiles-how-australian-children-are-using-mobile-phones

9 Elliot, J. (1978). *The Journals of Jim Elliot.* Ada, Michigan: Fleming H. Revell Company.

10 Muir, J. (1981). Ibid.

11 Einstein, A. (2009). *Cosmic Religion: With Other Opinions and Aphorisms.* New York: Dover Publications.

12 Martin, G.R.R. (2011). *A Dance with Dragons*. New York: Bantam Books.

13 Woolf, V. (1929). *A Room of One's Own*. London: Hogarth Press.

Chapter 7

1 Twenge, J.M., Martin, G.N., Campbell, W.K. (2018). Decreases in psychological well-being among American adolescents after 2012 and links to screen time during the rise of smartphone technology. *Emotion*, 18, 765–780.

2 Twenge, J.M., Haidt, J., Blake, A.B., McAllister, C., Lemon, H., LeRoy, A. (2021). Worldwide increases in adolescent loneliness. *Journal of Adolescence*, 93, 257–269.

3 Luo, Y., Liang, L., Zhou, H. et al. (2025). The impact of social media addiction on depression among university students in Wuhan, China: a longitudinal study. *BMC Public Health* 25, 2279. https://doi.org/10.1186/s12889-025-23443-3

4 Beneito López, P., Vicente-Chirivella, Ó. (2022). Banning mobile phones in schools: evidence from regional-level policies in Spain. *Applied Economic Analysis*, 30 (90): 153–175. https://doi.org/10.1108/AEA-05-2021-0112

5 Common Sense Media. (2023). The Common Sense Census: Media Use by Tweens and Teens, 2023.

6 Twenge, J.M. (2021). *iGen: Why Today's Super-Connected Kids Are Growing Up Less Rebellious, More Tolerant, and Less Happy*. New York: Atria Books.

7   World Health Organization. (2019). Gaming Disorder.
    https://www.who.int/news-room/questions-and-answers/
    item/addictive-behaviours-gaming-disorder

8   Royal College of Paediatrics and Child Health (RCPCH).
    (2019). The health impacts of screen time: a guide for clinicians
    and parents. https://opis-cdn.tinkoffjournal.ru/mercury/kids-
    psychiatry-doc1.xp3sfr..pdf?utm_source=chatgpt.com

9   Rogers, F. (n.d.). Quoted in multiple interviews and speeches.

10 Mental Health Research Canada. (2024). Youth Mental Health
    and Screen Time Report. https://www.mhrc.ca

11 Mah, J.K., Canadian Health Survey on Children and Youth
    (CHSCY). (2025). Associations between screen time and mental
    wellbeing among adolescents in Canada. *BMC Public Health*, 25,
    Article 874. https://doi.org/10.1186/s12889-025-22874-2

12 Canadian Paediatric Society. (2022). Screen time and
    preschool children: Promoting health and development in a
    digital world. https://cps.ca/en/documents/position/screen-
    time-and-preschool-children?utm_source=chatgpt.com

13 Beard, J. (1974). *Beard on Food: The Best Recipes and Kitchen
    Wisdom from the Dean of American Cooking.* New York: Alfred
    A. Knopf.

14 Dickens, C. (1860). *The Mystery of Edwin Drood.* (Attributed;
    quote paraphrased and commonly cited.)

15 Confucius. (Attributed; classical Chinese proverb widely
    credited to Confucius in educational and philosophical texts.)

16 Thoreau, H.D. (1863). *Journals of Henry David Thoreau.*
    New York: Houghton Mifflin.

17 Brown, B. (2010). *The Gifts of Imperfection: Let Go of Who You Think You're Supposed to Be and Embrace Who You Are*. Center City, Minnesota: Hazelden Publishing.

Chapter 8

1   Baer, D. (2015). 13 qualities Google looks for in job candidates. World Economic Forum, 29 April 2015. https://www.weforum.org/stories/2015/04/13-qualities-google-looks-for-in-job-candidates/
2   National Institutes of Health. (2022). Adolescent Brain Cognitive Development (ABCD) Study. https://abcdstudy.org
3   Garey, J. (2024). Teens and Sleep: The Cost of Sleep Deprivation. Child Mind Institute. https://childmind.org/article/happens-teenagers-dont-get-enough-sleep/
4   Perry, B.D., Szalavitz, M. (2006). *The Boy Who Was Raised as a Dog: And Other Stories from a Child Psychiatrist's Notebook*. New York: Basic Books.
5   Centre for Addiction and Mental Health (CAMH). (2023). Youth Mental Health Report. https://www.camh.ca/en/professionals/treatment/youth-mental-health
6   NHS Digital. (2023). Children's Health and Wellbeing Survey. https://digital.nhs.uk/data-and-information/publications/statistical/mental-health-of-children-and-young-people-in-england/2023-wave-4-follow-up
7   National Institutes of Health. (2022). Adolescent Brain Cognitive Development Study. https://abcdstudy.org

8 McNeill, J., Howard, S., Melhuish, E. (2024). Reducing screen time boosts children's mental health and prosocial behaviours. *Journal of Academic Medicine*. https://www.psypost.org/reducing-screen-time-boosts-childrens-mental-health-and-prosocial-behaviors-study-finds/

9 Daly-Smith, A., Smith, J.J., Lubans, D.R., Lonsdale, C., Riley, N., et al. (2025). Physical activity and cognitive functioning: A systematic review and meta-analysis. *British Journal of Sports Medicine*. https://bjsm.bmj.com/content/bjsports/early/2025/03/06/bjsports-2024-108589.full.pdf

10 McNeill, J., Howard, S., Melhuish, E. (2024). Loc. cit.

11 Walker, M. (2017). *Why We Sleep: Unlocking the Power of Sleep and Dreams*. New York: Scribner.

12 Kabat-Zinn, J. (1994). *Wherever You Go, There You Are: Mindfulness Meditation in Everyday Life*. New York: Hyperion.

13 Breuning, L.G. (2016). *The Science of Positivity: Stop Negative Thought Patterns by Changing Your Brain Chemistry*. New York: Simon & Schuster.

14 Dweck, C.S. (2006). *Mindset: The New Psychology of Success*. New York: Random House.

15 Ratey, J.J. (2008). *Spark: The Revolutionary New Science of Exercise and the Brain*. New York: Little, Brown.

16 University of South Australia. (2025). Exercise of any kind boosts brainpower at any age. https://www.unisa.edu.au/media-centre/Releases/2025/exercise-of-any-kind-boosts-brainpower-at-any-age/

17 University of South Australia. (2025). Loc. cit.

18 McNeill, J., Howard, S., Melhuish, E. (2024). Loc. cit.

Chapter 9

1   Walsh, T. (2024). *Faking It: Artificial Intelligence in a Human World*. Melbourne: Black Inc.

2   Vidal, Q., Vincent-Lancrin, S., Yun, H. (2023). Emerging governance of generative AI in education. OECD Digital Education Outlook 2023 Towards an Effective Digital Education Ecosystem. https://www.oecd.org/en/publications/ oecd-digital-education-outlook-2023_c74f03de-en/ full-report/emerging-governance-of-generative-ai-in-education_3cbd6269.html

3   MediaSmarts. (2023). Young Canadians in a Wireless World – Phase IV. https://mediasmarts.ca/ycww

4   Harvard Graduate School of Education. (2024). The Impact of AI on Children's Development. https://www. gse.harvard.edu/ideas/edcast/24/10/impact-ai-childrens-development

5   Masaryk, R. (2022). 41% of teenagers can't tell the difference between true and fake online health messages. *Frontiers in Psychology*. https://www.frontiersin.org/news/2022/08/29/ psychology-teenagers-health-fake-messages

6   Wang, Y., Kim, S., Li, J., Chen, L. (2025). Screen time and mental health outcomes among children and adolescents: Evidence from a nationally representative survey. *arXiv*. arXiv:2508.10062. https://arxiv.org/abs/2508.10062

7   Internetmatters.org. (2024). New research warns that many
    schools and parents are unprepared for the AI revolution.
    https://www.internetmatters.org/hub/press-release/ai-research-
    warns-schools-unprepared-artificial-intelligence/

8   Associated Press. (2024). Teens Are Turning to AI
    Companions for Support. https://apnews.com/article/
    ai-companion-generative-teens-mental-health-9ce59a2b250f3b
    d0187a717ffa2ad21f

9   Carson, R. (1965). *The Sense of Wonder*. New York: Harper &
    Row.

10 Lange, D. (n.d.). Quoted by the UC Berkeley School of
    Journalism. https://journalism.berkeley.edu

11 Voltaire. (1824). *A Philosophical Dictionary* (Vol. 1). London:
    Printed for J. and H.L. Hunt.

12 Drucker, P.F. (1999). *Management Challenges for the
    21st Century*. New York: HarperBusiness.

13 Franklin, B. (n.d.). Commonly attributed.

14 Barker, J.E., Semenov, A.D., Michaelson, L., Provan, L.S.,
    Snyder, H.R., Munakata, Y. (2014). Less-structured time
    in children's daily lives predicts self-directed executive
    functioning. *Frontiers in Psychology*, 5, 593. https://doi.
    org/10.3389/fpsyg.2014.00593

A final word

1   Dewey, J. (1926). My Pedagogic Creed. *The Journal of
    Education*, Vol. 104, No. 21.

Acknowledgements

This book is the result of countless conversations, questions and moments of reflection, and it would not exist without the support and insight of many generous souls.

First and foremost, to our closest friends and family who spent endless hours reading, editing and discussing our writing. Your patience, encouragement and unwavering belief in our work kept us grounded and inspired.

To our literary agent, Daniel Pilkington, thank you for championing this book, and Tanya for your editing skills. Your guidance and support made this project possible.

We are grateful to the editorial team at Simon & Schuster: Emma Nolan, Rosemary McDonald, Michelle Swainson and Rod Morrison. Your editorial wisdom, sharp eyes and commitment to this message elevated every chapter. You helped us speak not just clearly, but courageously.

To the students, parents, teachers, researchers, friends, colleagues and mentors who have challenged our thinking, shared their stories and reminded us why this work matters. Thank you. Your lived experience and fierce dedication to children's wellbeing have shaped this book in ways we can never fully repay.

This is not just our book; it's a collective effort, born from community, concern and hope. We're honoured to be part of the conversation.

Mark and Gavin

About the authors

Dr Mark A. Williams worked at MIT in the US, which is where the internet first started. It was a time when Facebook was only accessible to select university students and the first iPhone had just hit the market. Dr Mark watched in disbelief as students played 'Hot or Not', the precursor to social media, where male students ranked the attractiveness of female students. And he continued to watch as governments around the world failed to protect our most vulnerable. He is a professor of cognitive neuroscience and recently published a consensus statement with over one hundred internationally recognised experts on the effects of devices on children. He's also a dad to two wonderfully connected teenagers who have never had social media accounts.

Gavin McCormack has spent almost three decades teaching children across the globe as a Montessori-trained educator, witnessing firsthand the effect that environment, content and technology have on developing minds. He has built schools, libraries and teacher training centres in remote communities, and co-founded Upschool.co to give children everywhere free, purpose-driven learning that equips them for life beyond the classroom. His work has been recognised internationally, including being named one of the world's top ten most influential educators five years running, and he has spoken on the TEDx stage about how education can change the world. As the Montessori Australia Ambassador, Gavin works with schools and families to help children grow into resilient, curious and socially responsible adults. Above all, he has seen what happens when we give children the right conditions to thrive, and what happens when we don't.